Slow and Steady
Parenting

Slow and Steady Parenting

Active Child-Raising for the Long Haul
(Birth to Age Three)

CATHERINE A. SANDERSON

M. Evans
Lanham • Boulder • New York • Toronto • Oxford

Published by M. Evans
An imprint of The Rowman & Littlefield Publishing Group, Inc.
4501 Forbes Boulevard, Suite 200, Lanham, Maryland 20706

Designed and typeset by Chrissy Kwasnik

Distributed by NATIONAL BOOK NETWORK

Library of Congress Cataloging-in-Publication Data
Sanderson, Catherine Ashly, 1968–
    Slow and steady parenting : active child-raising for the long haul
 (birth to age 3) / Catherine A Sanderson.
        p. cm.
    Includes bibliographical references.
    ISBN-10: 1-59077-045-5
    ISBN-13: 978-1-59077-045-0
 1. Child rearing. 2. Parenting. 3. Parent and child. I. Title.
 HQ769.S2564 2005
 649'.122—dc22   2005011506

⊗™ The paper used in this publication meets the minimum requirements
of American National Standard for Information Sciences—Permanence of
Paper for Printed Library Materials, ANSI/NISO Z39.48-1992.

Manufactured in the United States of America.

In memory of Kim Morgan-Ebling,
one of the best mothers in the world.

CONTENTS

PART 3 The Third Year

PART 4 Special Issues Across the Years

ACKNOWLEDGMENTS

Writing a book is truly a process, and one that is impossible to complete without considerable assistance from many others. Therefore I wish to acknowledge these contributions and express my gratitude to various people. My agent, Jim Levine, who truly understood my initial vision for this book, provided thoughtful and constructive guidance in developing the initial proposal, persevered in finding this book a publisher, and helped guide me through the revision process. My editor, PJ Dempsey, who taught me the difference between academic and trade writing, provided specific and detailed comments on all drafts, and allowed me the space to find my own vision for this book. Mary Boughton, editorial assistant, for looking at the manuscript with a fresh eye and creating new and (vastly) improved headings. Darren Yopyk, my research assistant and friend, conducted numerous literature searches, gathered statistics, and even helped watch my own children while I frantically wrote. Many family members and friends generously shared their own parenting stories—good and bad—with me, which helped me flesh out my ideas with specific, concrete, and real life examples. My husband, Bart Hollander, believed in this project from the very beginning, allowed me to practice these ideas on our boys, and provided countless hours of childcare on weekends so I could write this book. And, last but not least, Andrew, Robert, and Caroline were the unknowing "guinea pigs" on whom virtually all of these ideas were tried.

PREFACE

After the birth of my first child in 1998, I eagerly looked for books that would help guide me through all of the child rearing decisions I was faced with:

Should I breast-feed or formula feed?

Should my child use a pacifier or suck his thumb?

How can I get my son to sleep at 4 AM?

How can I get my child to eat healthy foods?

How can I avoid embarrassing tantrums in public places?

And although I consulted many parenting guides, I felt really frustrated with the information I read. First, I wanted guidance that was based on current scientific research so that I could be sure the choices I made as a parent were good—physically and emotionally—for my child. But many of the leading self-help parenting books are written by child psychologists or pediatricians who received their education and training some time ago—and we know a lot more today about child rearing than we did twenty and thirty years ago. For example, for many years people thought formula feeding was safer and healthier than breast-feeding, and therefore only women who couldn't financially afford formula chose to nurse their infants. Of course we know now that breast-feeding is much better for babies (and their moms) than formula feeding, and hence virtually all women are encouraged to give nursing a try. Even as recently as ten years ago parents were told to put babies to sleep on their stomachs as a way of avoiding having the baby spit up during the night and potentially choke. But research has shown that babies who sleep on their stomachs are at a greater risk of experiencing sudden infant death syndrome (SIDS), and parents are now told that babies should be put to sleep on their backs. I therefore wanted current, scientifically-based information so that I could make informed decisions about my many child rearing challenges.

I also found that many of the leading child rearing guides were written by people who haven't actively parented their own children in many, many years. Although these experts may have received considerable education and training in issues of child development, typically either as a pediatrician or psychologist, I wasn't sure about their ability to provide practical strategies for handling all the challenges I was facing every day (and night). Could I really trust the advice of a pediatrician, who would only see a child a few times a year for brief office visits, for guidance in how to make crucial day to day choices in how to raise my child? I frankly didn't see how such a person could give me concrete advice about my most pressing issues, such as how to get my child to sleep, how to handle temper tantrums, and how to get my child to eat healthy foods. I wanted specific and practical advice from a parent who was now in—or had recently been in—"the trenches," namely, facing the precise child rearing challenges I was facing.

Because I am a researcher by training, I started looking in scientific journals in medicine and psychology for advice about making various child rearing choices. And I was surprised—and pleased—to find that experts in both the fields of medicine and psychology had largely reached the same conclusions regarding the two major goals that virtually all parents have, namely, how to help their children's psychological and physical well-being. This reading led me to develop a unique approach to parenting—one that helps babies and toddlers develop into happy and healthy children, and makes parents' already hectic lives easier in numerous ways. Because this approach focuses on taking a long-term perspective to major child rearing challenges, and avoiding the often tempting quick-fix solutions, I call this perspective *slow and steady parenting*.

In this book, I will show how to discard short-term, quick-fix approaches and replace them with a scientifically-based, long-term approach that can be applied to most child rearing challenges faced by parents of infants and toddlers, including breast-feeding, using a pacifier, eating, sleeping, and toilet training. Is this a revolutionary view of human behavior? Not at all. As adults, we often make long-term choices, even when the short-term choices are very appealing. Deciding not to order dessert is making the long-term choice to avoid weight gain, even when the short-term choice to enjoy the taste of cheesecake is tempting. Deciding to stay late at the office several nights, or even weeks, in a row while working on an important project is making a long-term choice to advance your career, even when the short term choice to get home early and relax is quite desirable. Deciding to put your paycheck in the bank is making the long-term choice to save money for next summer's vacation, even when the short-term choice of purchasing a fancy watch or flat-screen television is very appealing. We adults (usually) understand that even very tempting short-term choices can have negative long-term consequences. This book is therefore based on a very simple and straightforward premise, namely that quick-fix solutions to many child rearing challenges often have hidden consequences—I've simply taken what we all know about making important choices in life, and have applied this perspective to making important choices in child rearing.

HOW BEST TO USE THIS BOOK

I've divided the chapters of this book into distinct parts to help parents guide their reading. Because children present different challenges at different ages, these parts are loosely organized by the child's age:

Part 1 addresses the challenges of the first year (breast versus bottle feeding, sleeping, and pacifier use);

Part 2 addresses the challenges of the second year (eating, television, and play);

Part 3 addresses the challenges of the third year (toilet training, discipline, and learning new skills); and

Part 4 addresses two specific challenges parents of infants and toddlers face (finding childcare, managing family spacing) and provides specific advice for extending the slow and steady approach as the child grows.

It is my hope that this organization will help parents focus on the chapters they are likely to find most useful at a given time. Although the slow and steady perspective is based in scientific research (mostly from psychology and medicine), I didn't want to disrupt the flow of the book with lots of references to specific studies. But for those interested, I've provided references to the major studies in the reference section at the end of the book.

FOR NEW PARENTS AND PARENTS-TO-BE

If you are a new parent or a parent-to-be, first of all, congratulations! Parenting is by far the most challenging but rewarding job I've ever had. I hope that this book will give you some insight into many of the major child rearing challenges that you'll face during the infant and toddler years, and hopefully make your transition to the exciting world of parenting that much easier.

The first section of this book will probably be most helpful to you right now. In this section I address the major issues parents face early on in their parenting lives, including breast-feeding versus bottle-feeding, getting your baby to sleep, and whether to give your baby a pacifier. If your baby has not yet arrived, this information can be especially helpful in giving you some pointers for managing the very early days and weeks. You also might turn to the fourth section, where I describe how slow and steady parenting can be applied to specific child rearing challenges that many parents face at some point in their child's first few years: finding childcare and managing family spacing.

FOR EXPERIENCED PARENTS

If you are like most experienced parents I know, you probably aren't even reading this introductory chapter, given the many demands on your time. But if you are, my advice is to read the chapters that will provide you with specific strategies for coping with the major challenges you are currently facing. If you have a picky eater, read Chapter 4 (Healthy Eating). If you have a baby who is waking up several times throughout the night, turn to Chapter 2 (The Bedtime Challenge). The index also provides an easy way to reference particular topics (e.g., sibling relationships, videos, dessert) that are addressed within individual chapters. And if you ever do have some "spare time," read the section of the book that fits with your child's age—you might even learn some strategies for avoiding future problems.

INTRODUCING SLOW
AND STEADY PARENTING

The slow and steady parenting approach is based in the classic children's story about the tortoise and the hare, in which the quick running hare leads the race for many, many miles, but ultimately the slow and steady approach of the tortoise wins the race. In parenting this means that, like the tortoise, it's better to take the slower route when dealing with the day-to-day trials and tribulations of raising a child. To put it bluntly, the quick term fixes, what I call short-term solutions, often lead to long-term consequences.

The slow and steady approach to child rearing is based in the belief that out of some combination of ignorance and desperation, many parents make short-term choices to common child rearing challenges simply because these quick-fixes are easier at the moment. We choose bottle-feeding over breast-feeding because we want to avoid the inconvenience of breast-feeding. We put a pacifier in our baby's mouth when she is sad because that is the easiest way to provide comfort at the moment. You buy your toddler a lollipop at the grocery store because you are desperate to avoid an embarrassing fit. All of the choices are made frequently by caring and dedicated parents, who believe they are making good choices for the child—and for themselves. And these choices indeed help you in the short-term to get more sleep, minimize tears, and avoid a tantrum.

But parents who make such short-term choices are overlooking the long-term consequences of these quick-fixes both for their children and themselves. You may be willing to rock your one-month-old to sleep several times a night, but may tire of this lengthy routine by the time the child is four-months-old. You may be willing to feed dessert to your one-year-old each night as a way of getting some calories in him, but then feel alarmed when you learn he is considered obese at age three. You may be thrilled to have the chance to read the newspaper while your toddler watches *Stanley* each morning, but feel dismayed when your first grader comes home from school each day and wants to watch television instead of play outside or build with Legos. In sum, relying on such short-term choices may be easier at the moment, but can lead to long-term consequences.

STROLLER USE—AND ABUSE: AN EXAMPLE OF SLOW AND STEADY PARENTING IN ACTION

An easy example of a common quick-fix for many parents is the use of strollers for kids who can, and should, walk. Strollers were intended originally for carting around infants and very young children who don't yet walk, but an increasingly large number of parents are now using strollers for their three and even four-year-old children. Parents choose to use strollers for their own convenience—let's face it, a stroller lets the parents walk faster (because shorter legs do walk more slowly than longer legs), but consider the downside. It deprives children of interesting stimulation like taking time to look at a flower or a crack in the sidewalk or anything else that captures their attention. This is a classic example of a short-term parenting choice—stroller use makes it easier for parents to run errands quickly without worrying about keeping track of wandering children, and using a stroller helps accomplish these tasks.

Unfortunately, the long-term consequences of this decision to keep an already walking child confined to a stroller means depriving a toddler of important opportunities to practice movement and explore their environment, which in turn fosters physical and intellectual development. Preschool children need active exploration with their environment. Toddlers are perfecting their walking (and running) skills, and want to investigate everything around them closely. Yet it is impossible to jump in a puddle or spy a tiny insect on a leaf while being pushed rapidly in a stroller. Furthermore, three- and four-year-old children enjoy jumping, hopping, and skipping—all behaviors that are more appropriate for the outdoors. If you confine preschoolers to a stroller, you deprive them of important opportunities to explore the world, practice new skills, and exercise independent choice. Moreover, after a long stroller walk, parents are tired from pushing the stroller but kids get home with lots of energy—a very bad combination!

In contrast, you can make the long-term choice to let your toddler walk, which allows him to actively engage in the world and practice newly-acquired physical skills. Sure, it will be slower for you, but your child will experience lasting benefits, and you may even benefit by, literally, taking time to smell the roses.

HOW SLOW AND STEADY PARENTING HELPS YOUR CHILD

Making long-term choices leads to long-term advantages for three reasons:

1. It creates children who are firmly attached to you. Children benefit from this type of responsive parenting because they feel their needs are understood and are met in a direct way. A child will be disappointed when a parent won't buy the highly desired Lego firetruck right away, but tells the child that it will be added to their birthday wish list—but he or she will also understand that you have paid attention to the request and may indeed buy the toy at a later time. In contrast, quick-fix choices often mean ignoring your child's needs, and thereby interfere with the formation of a secure attachment bond. A child who is ignored while he or she cries at night alone in their bed, for example, learns that you are not willing or able to comfort them at a time of need.

2. It creates children who have a strong sense of mastery and independence. The long-term approach focuses on teaching your child important life skills so that he or she develops independence and self-reliance. For example, if you help your child learn strategies for getting him or herself to sleep, you are giving your child valuable tools for mastering this important developmental challenge. In contrast, relying on quick-fix choices can disrupt the formation of a strong sense of independence and self-reliance. A child who is simply given a pacifier to calm himself down can fail to develop his own self-soothing strategies.

3. It creates children who are more physically fit and healthy. A long-term approach focuses on making child raising choices that benefit your child's physical health. Children who are breast-fed, for example, experience a number of health benefits, including lower rates of ear infections, leukemia, and SIDS. Similarly, children who learn strategies for entertaining themselves in an active way are at a lower risk of developing obesity. In contrast, quick-fix choices may seem good to you initially, but can lead to numerous long-term consequences. Children who are given a bottle in their cribs, for example, are at an increased risk of developing tooth decay, asthma, and ear infections, and children who spend hours in front of the television are at greater risk of developing obesity as well as attention problems.

Child psychologists Edward Christophersen and Susan Mortweet describe their own long-term approach to parenting as developing a "ten-year plan." In other words, they believe that you should use your time and energy to help your child become the person you want him or her to be not right at the moment, but rather in ten years. If you allow your preschooler to watch television every day, you may be pleased with who the person is right at the moment—because he or she is focusing on the screen and not interrupting you—but you may be considerably less happy when your thirteen-year-old comes home from school every day and insists on watching television instead of engaging in more active forms of play. They recommend, and I wholeheartedly agree with their approach, that parents need to make choices about developmental tasks with a focus on helping your child learn the skills you'd like him or her to have in the future.

HOW SLOW AND STEADY PARENTING SIMPLIFIES YOUR LIFE

I'm a mother of three and as a parent, I find myself constantly struggling to do all that is needed to care for my family and myself—doing the laundry, washing the dishes, paying the bills, buying presents for the frequent birthday parties my kids attend, taking the dog to the vet, and so on. So I'm looking for specific parenting approaches that will simplify my life—I don't want to fight the same battles with my kids day after day, and I don't want to create bad habits in my kids that ultimately will cost me time and energy as I try to undo them. In short, the slow and steady parenting approach helps you:

1. Avoid many of the common parent-child struggles. These struggles concern such issues as eating, toilet training, and pacifier use. Avoiding giving your baby a pacifier, for example, means you never have to figure out ways to take away the pacifier as your child gets older.

2. Save time and energy. When applied consistently, this long-term approach saves time and energy—in part because you are teaching your child a life skill as opposed to simply doing for your child. For example, teaching your baby how to fall asleep on his or her own will free you from spending your evenings falling asleep in your child's bed.

TEACHING SLOW AND STEADY PARENTING TO YOUR CHILD'S OTHER CAREGIVERS

Because most of us rely at least occasionally on other people to take care of our kids, teaching these caregivers about the slow and steady approach is a good idea. It provides a consistent routine that is beneficial to your child's development. Decide on the choices that feel right to you and your partner, and then convey those same choices to all caregivers (e.g., babysitters, nannies, grandparents, etc.). Just think about how confusing it would be if your baby throws a fit on an outing with grandmother and then receives a pacifier, but not when such a fit occurs when he or she is with you. Similarly, if a babysitter rocks your baby to sleep one time, he or she will then expect this treatment each and every time. If grandmother permits an afternoon of watching videos, your child will expect a similar plan the next time your mother babysits. On the other hand, if your child understands that all caregivers follow the same routine and have the same expectations, their world will become predictable and secure. Kids have an easier time adjusting to and feeling comfortable with different caregivers who all respect the same rules.

Part 1

THE FIRST YEAR

Chapter 1
Breast-Feeding

How to feed your baby is one of the first decisions you'll make as a parent, and it's a perfect example of the difference between making a short-term choice versus a long-term choice. As you'll see, there are pros and cons to both breast-feeding and bottle-feeding from a practical, and short-term, point of view. But the long-term advantages of nursing make breast-feeding truly the best choice. Will it always be easy? No. It will take dedication and a reordering of your life, but you and your child will both reap the psychological, physical, and emotional benefits, both now and for a long time to come.

WHAT THE EXPERTS SAY

Breast-feeding is the most natural and healthy way to feed your baby—that's why both the American Academy of Pediatrics and the American Dietetic Association recommend that moms nurse for one year. And the longer you breast-feed, the more your child benefits, meaning that babies who are breast-fed for twelve months experience more benefits than those who are breast-fed for six months, who in turn benefit more than those who are breast-fed for three months, and so on. No matter what you might hear, breast milk provides the very best nutrition. I'm telling you this so that you can resist pressure from those around you who might still harbor old wives' tales from the past, and who insist formula feeding is better—or even the same. We've all heard well-meaning family members and friends say "Well, I didn't breast-feed and my child turned out just fine," which is another subtle (or not so subtle) way of implying that breast-feeding is not necessary.

WHY FORMULA FEEDING HAS LONG-TERM CONSEQUENCES

Although formula feeding is often seen, especially by new moms, as the easiest way to feed your baby, this decision has a number of long-term consequences.

Formula feeding leads to poorer health for baby. Because only breast-feeding provides your baby with important antibodies from you that fight illness and disease, babies who are formula fed are more likely to develop various minor illnesses such as diarrhea, urinary tract infections, gastrointestinal disease, vomiting, respiratory infections, coughing and wheezing, and ear infections. What's more, bottle-fed babies are at higher risk of developing major health problems, including cancer, coronary heart disease, meningitis, sudden infant death syndrome (SIDS), pneumonia, and leukemia.

In turn, and not surprisingly, formula fed babies have more pediatrician visits than breast-fed babies. And taking a sick child to the pediatrician is pretty inconvenient—calling to make the appointment, going to the appointment, waiting to be seen, filling the prescription, forcing your child to take medicine, and so on. My children were all breast-fed for one year and in that time, my older son experienced a single ear infection (necessitating one pediatrician visit) and my younger two kids never had a sick baby doctor visit. In contrast, my friends who formula fed their children were at the doctor monthly. Check around with your friends—you'll find similar stories.

Formula-feeding disrupts the attachment bond. When you give your baby a bottle, you typically don't hold the baby as close to you as if you are breast-feeding, simply because the bottle can be held at some distance away from your body, whereas breasts are obviously attached to your body. Moreover, formula-feeding rarely, if ever, involves such intimate physical contact between you and your baby, including close skin-to-skin contact, which we know makes an important contribution to infant attachment. For example, premature infants who receive skin-to-skin contact with their parents develop stronger attachment bonds than those who don't experience this type of touch. Premature infants who receive this type of "skin-to-skin" contact with their mothers cry less, gain more weight, and experience deeper sleep compared to those who receive standard care. They are also released from the hospital faster.

WHAT YOU REALLY NEED TO KNOW ABOUT BREAST-FEEDING—BUT NO ONE EVER TOLD YOU

Despite all of the health benefits of breast-feeding for babies, most moms breast-feed for only a short time if at all. Only 67.2 percent of mothers ever try breast-feeding, 47 percent are breast-feeding seven days after birth, 32 percent are breast-feeding at two months, 19 percent at four months, and 10 percent at six months. Why do so few women choose to nurse, or stop nursing so soon? Simply put, breast-feeding is not something that happens in a completely easy and magical way—it takes some time to get used to.

Breast-feeding takes time. Let's face it—breast-feeding can be considered an inconvenience. At the most basic level, choosing formula means that other people can feed your baby. Very young infants typically eat every two to three hours, and this means you simply can't be away from your baby for more than about an hour. The most common reasons women choose to use formula is because they need to be away from the baby for a day or more at a time—they may need to travel for work, attend a wedding in a different state, or simply want to sleep through the night. Although keeping a supply of breast milk in the fridge provides nursing mothers some opportunity to be away from their infant for longer periods of time, pumping milk in and of itself is time consuming—and is still a task that of course can only be performed by the mother! Simply pouring formula into a bottle so that your children can be fed by any willing caregiver, certainly seems more convenient, but it's not convenient later in life when you wished you had more of a bond with your child.

Breast-feeding gets easier over time. Breast-feeding, at least at the beginning, can be painful. Even infants without teeth have a strong ability to suck, and because in the first few weeks they may nurse eight to ten times a day, your nipples can quickly become very sore. I have friends who report wincing every time their infant "latched on," due to the initial sharp pain. But don't let this deter you. It's a minor inconvenience that will pass in a short time. If you have the patience to continue, I promise you will thank me as you begin to enjoy this very special bond with your baby—a bond that will serve you both well for years to come.

WHY BREAST-FEEDING HAS LONG-TERM ADVANTAGES

For Babies

The slow and steady approach to feeding your baby focuses on the psychological as well as physical benefits of breast-feeding for babies—there's simply no better way to provide your baby with the best start on a lifetime of physical, mental, and emotional health.

Breast-fed babies are more intelligent. Infants who are breast-fed have higher IQs and higher scores on tests of cognitive development as well as vocabulary later on than those who are bottle-fed. Yes, it's true. Infants who were breast-fed for six or more months scored higher on a vocabulary test at age five—8.2 points higher for females and 5.8 points higher for males. What leads to the greater intelligence in breast-fed babies? One study found that nursing is associated with increases in brain activity of newborns, which also occurs during bottle-feeding but to a less intense degree. Infants are also more interactive with their environment immediately after breast-feeding—for example, they pay greater attention to a mobile—whereas formula fed babies do not show such a benefit. What better long-term advantage could you want for your child than to give him the best head start you can in life?

Breast-fed babies learn to naturally control their eating. A lot of research has examined the connection between formula-feeding and obesity, and this is what we now know to be true: Bottle-fed babies are often fed a set amount of formula each day, and the focus is to get the baby to eat the "right amount." Breast-fed babies, on the other hand, learn how to regulate how much they take in because moms have no idea how much they are drinking. They stop nursing when they've had enough. In turn, breast-fed babies are 16 percent less likely to be overweight and 37 percent less likely to be obese than those who are formula fed.

Breast-fed babies tend to be better eaters as toddlers and children. Another reason for the higher rates of obesity in formula fed babies is that babies who are exposed to only one taste via formula for their first few months are less tolerant of trying different foods later on in life—which can lead to more limited taste preferences and in turn a less balanced and nutritious diet. In contrast, breast-fed babies have early exposure to a variety of different types of tastes because they've had a weakened taste of whatever food their mother consumed via her breast milk.

Breast-feeding allows babies to fulfill their intense sucking needs without taking in additional calories. A baby who is nursing can get all of the comfort from sucking that he needs because sucking on an empty breast doesn't mean overeating. Bottle-fed babies, on the other hand, can't suck without feeding and therefore will eat more than they need to, or will want a pacifier (learn more about the drawbacks of pacifier use in Chapter 4).

Breast-feeding enhances the attachment bond. Not only does the act of breast-feeding help your baby develop a stronger and more intense bond with you, the breast-feeding position allows for close skin-to-skin connection and good eye contact. Moms who breast-feed show greater affection towards their babies during feeding than those who are formula feeding. This means that breast-fed babies must be held while eating—just think about how often you see formula fed babies sitting alone and holding their own bottles.

For Moms

The slow and steady approach to feeding your baby also has real and lasting benefits for moms—it's good for our physical and psychological health, and most importantly, it simplifies our lives.

Breast-feeding is good for mom's physical health. Lots of research has examined the physical effects of breast-feeding for moms—and it all consistently shows that breast-feeding leads to many health benefits. First, the hormone oxytocin is released into the bloodstream during nursing, which speeds up the shrinking of the uterus and hence decreases postpartum bleeding and anemia. Breast-feeding is also a great way to lose the dreaded pregnancy weight—nursing moms burn an extra half pound of fat each week (and if that's not an easy way to burn fat, I don't know what is). Breast-feeding mothers also have fewer minor illnesses, such as colds, respiratory infections, and gastrointestinal infections. And if you've ever felt sick while needing to care for a small child, you know just how important staying healthy is. Finally, the physical benefits of breast-feeding for you, as with those for your baby, are quite long-lasting—women who breast-feed are less likely to develop breast cancer, ovarian and endometrial cancer, arthritis, and osteoporosis.

Breast-feeding is good for mom's psychological health. In addition to the physical benefits, breast-feeding also provides numerous psychological benefits for you. Women who breast-feed experience lower levels of stress, anxiety, and depression than do those who choose to formula feed. Once again, the hormone oxytocin seems to be responsible for this effect—it influences brain chemistry to create a soothing, antidepressant effect. Stress related hormones are twice as high in women who are formula-feeding compared to those who are breast-feeding. And what new mother isn't desperate to reduce levels of stress and anxiety?

Breast-feeding simplifies your life. With nursing, the milk is at the right temperature, it is the right amount, it is already mixed, and it doesn't need to be sterilized. When I'm nursing and it is the middle of the night, I have to get up—or, better yet, have my husband get up and bring the baby to me—but then I'm ready to nurse. Would it be more convenient to wake up, go to the kitchen, find a bottle, pour in formula, heat it to the right temperature (not using the microwave), find a nipple, check the temperature, and then bring it back to the baby? I never have to go to the store, I never have to sterilize bottles and nipples, and I never have to buy formula. When I'm with friends who have chosen to formula-feed, I'm always amazed at the amount of work it is—breast-feeding is just so much simpler. Taking care of a baby is complicated enough without making it more so, especially since nature has provided a superior alternative.

Breast-feeding can lead to mom pampering. Although money alone shouldn't be the reason for breast-feeding, it certainly is a dramatically cheaper way of feeding your baby than formula. So, if you think breast-feeding would be too inconvenient or awkward, imagine what you could do with the money you'd save—how about having a pedicure twice a month, hiring a babysitter for a few hours every week, or taking a weekend trip?

THE SLOW AND STEADY APPROACH

Breast-Feeding

Now that you know how breast-feeding can benefit you and your baby in the long-term, use the following steps to make this a totally positive experience for you both.

1. Make the decision to breast-feed, and start breast-feeding immediately after delivery.

Breast-feeding doesn't happen by accident—if you want to breast-feed, you need to commit to doing it prior to delivery and tell your obstetrician, midwife, and nurses of your intentions. You should try to nurse shortly after delivery—the American Academy of Pediatrics recommends in the first hour after birth—and, if at all possible, to have your baby room-in with you. If your baby is staying in the nursery, you simply won't know when your baby needs to nurse. Moreover, in some nurseries babies are routinely offered formula, bottles of sugar water, and/or pacifiers, all of which can interfere with your ability to establish a nursing routine. In fact, a study in the *Journal of the American Medical Association* found that babies who roomed-in were breast-fed much more frequently than those who were cared for in the nursery—and, not surprisingly, babies who roomed-in gained more weight and were less likely to require formula supplementation.

Even if you aren't totally committed to breast-feeding, remember that you can always start to breast-feed and then switch to formula feeding. But you can't do the reverse because your breasts will no longer be making milk.

2. Don't give your baby pacifiers or bottles at all for the first three to six weeks.

Breast-feeding is a learning process for both you and your baby, and introducing other sources of sucking can interfere with the establishment of good nursing. Sucking on artificial nipples and pacifiers requires a baby to learn different motions and can impair the ability to nurse from a real nipple. Although I'd avoid the use of pacifiers forever (see Chapter 3), bottle-feeding can be introduced after nursing is well-established (usually between three to six weeks). It's true that bottle-feeding does afford greater convenience for mothers, especially because it allows the involvement of other caregivers, so if you are willing to pump (see point #4 below), your baby can experience the health benefits of breast milk while being bottle-fed occasionally by others. But if you want to be able to use a bottle (for formula and/or breast milk) during your baby's first year, don't wait too long—an infant who has no exposure to bottles prior to eight or ten weeks old may resist this change completely!

3. Don't feed "supplemental" bottles of formula.

Even if you are breast-feeding, you may think about giving your baby formula at times, perhaps when you must be at work or during the middle of the night when you'd prefer to sleep. But the problem with supplementing with formula is that your body produces the amount of milk it believes your baby needs—so if you are feeding your baby supplemental bottles, your milk supply will decrease proportionately and over time, will actually decrease to the point where you'll *need* to provide bottles of formula. As you can see, feeding supplemental formula starts a vicious cycle—often leading to complete weaning. We also know from considerable scientific research that supplementing with formula is simply not as good as always feeding breast milk. So, what do you do when you must be away from your baby, or simply must get a good night's sleep?

4. Pump and store your breast milk.

There will definitely be times when your baby will need to eat and you won't be around—this means you'll have to make sure you have a quantity of break milk stored for such times. Buying a good quality breast pump, ideally an electric one that enables both breasts to be pumped at the same time, will make this easier. Although they can be expensive ($200-$250), many hospitals have breast pumps for rent, which can be a good alternative. And if you balk at that cost, just think about the money you'll save on formula. If you don't have access to an electric pump, don't let that stop you from using a manual pump. Manual pumps are getting better all the time, and many women find these pumps just as easy to use—they just take a little bit more time.

5. Find specific ways to involve spouses, partners, and grandparents in baby care.

Don't choose to stop breast-feeding, or never start breast-feeding, because you think it will deprive partners or other family members of much needed involvement with the infant. There are many alternative ways for caregivers to be involved in infant care, particularly during the first few weeks when it is best not to introduce bottles. My husband and I agreed that I'd handle putting the food in and he could handle dealing with the food output—changing diapers—which seemed like a great deal to me! My mother especially enjoyed bathing my children, and almost everyone loves having the opportunity to rock, sing, and read to babies. And if you have a breast pump, it is easy to give caregivers a chance to feed a bottle—just wait for a few weeks to make sure breast-feeding is going smoothly. You might even choose to regularly pump in the late evening, so your partner can give the baby a middle-of-the-night bottle.

6. Learn the correct way to breast-feed.

As I've said, breast-feeding is not immediately natural or in-tuitive to most women—as with many new skills, this one takes practice. One of the best things you can do is to take a class in breast-feeding prior to the birth of your baby. Many hospitals offer such training and if you are already taking a class in childbirth, why not add a class in lactation? Even one two- to three-hour class can teach you various ways to hold your baby during nursing, how to establish a good "latch on" position, and strategies for coping with sore nipples. Learning the right way to breast-feed can go a long way to reducing some of the common problems of soreness in the first few weeks.

7. Talk to a lactation consultant if/when you need it.

Breast-feeding in the beginning can be painful—vigorous sucking by a hungry infant on a sensitive body part can lead to soreness and even pain. Although this soreness tends to peak in the first few weeks as the nipples get used to this new—and constant—stimulation, you may continue to have problems with cracking and bleeding, which in turn can lead to a rapid decision to switch to formula. If you experience any substantial discomfort from nursing, contact a lactation consultant (ask your pediatrician or obstetrician for recommendations—or refer to the appendix for a list of helpful books and organizations). This service is often free or covered by health insurance, and even a phone consultation can provide some good strategies for alleviating the pain.

8. Find creative ways to balance work and nursing.

Breast-feeding and a full-time job can be compatible with some thought and planning. First, most of us have a few months of maternity leave, and since nursing is more frequent for very young babies than older ones, try to continue to work as close to your due date as possible. This way you can use your maternity leave to care for the baby and not to prepare for the birth. Once your maternity leave is over, see if you can initially return to work on a part-time basis, and/or arrange to work from home for some period of time. Because babies begin to eat solid food when they are between four and six month old, nursing frequency can decrease by around six months. Most six-month-old babies will only need to nurse four times a day, so a woman who works outside the home can nurse before she leaves for work, pump during her lunch hour (to provide milk for the next day's lunch) nurse again immediately after work, and nurse at bedtime. This means having to pump only once a day from work. If you work close to your home, near your child's daycare center, or have a caregiver with a flexible schedule, you could alternatively arrange to nurse during your lunch hour and thereby eliminate the middle of the day pumping.

9. Find ways to nurse in public situations.

Because one of the reasons some women stop nursing—or never nurse to begin with—is their concern about breast-feeding in public situations, develop a plan for feeding your baby in public situations that works for you. Some women choose to not nurse at all in public, and instead pump breast milk ahead of time so they can simply feed a bottle in these situations. Other women find appropriate public places in which they can nurse—I always had great luck going into a maternity or children's clothing store and asking if I could sit in a dressing room to nurse. Depending on where you live, some department stores and grocery stores may even have private areas for nursing mothers.

Maternity stores often sell specially-designed garments that allow private nursing in public places through carefully designed flaps and buttons.

Formula Feeding

If you are unable to breast-feed for any reason, there are ways to bottle-feed that can impart some of the same long-term physical and psychological benefits of breast-feeding for you and your baby.

1. Always hold your baby during feedings.

Hold your baby each and every time you feed so that you maintain the type of close physical and eye contact that breast-fed babies automatically receive. Don't deprive your bottle-fed baby of this type of contact. Bottles should never be propped up so that an infant is feeding alone, nor should they be given to older babies who are able to hold a bottle on their own.

2. Whenever possible, allow close skin-to-skin contact during feeding.

Skin-to-skin contact while giving your baby a bottle creates a strong attachment bond. When possible, remove your shirt when feeding your baby a bottle. This is also a great strategy for fathers to use to develop a closer bond with their baby. Parents who have skin-to-skin contact with their infants show greater attachment to them as well as greater confidence in caring for them.

3. Let your baby control how much he or she is eating.

Trust me—you don't get a prize for giving your baby the maximum amount of formula he or she will drink in a single feeding. When your baby loses interest in sucking during a feeding, this is a good sign that your baby is full. Let your baby control how much, and understand that a child may eat more at some feedings than at others. It is OK if some formula is wasted—it will help you get used to the tremendous amount of food that toddlers waste when they spread it on their clothes, in their hair, and on the walls.

Chapter 2
The Bedtime Challenge

Ask one hundred new parents to list their toughest parent-ing challenges, and I guarantee that getting their baby (and themselves) to sleep is on the top of that list. Learning the slow and steady approach to sleep is very important because how you handle bedtime is critical—this event is one of those crucial times in which you have an opportunity to choose long-term solutions that both shape your baby's psychological development and simplify your own life.

GETTING YOUR BABY TO SLEEP

At the end of a long day, we are very eager for our down time and getting baby to sleep is a major step toward achieving that goal. The hour or two or even (dare to dream) three that we can spend relaxing with our partner, or talking on the phone, or reading a book without interruption is crucial to our well-being. We also know what happens the next day when we have an overly tired and very grumpy baby (or partner). Our desire to get our baby to sleep can lead us to do "whatever it takes." Desperate for some down time, we are tempted to resort to whatever method seems to be working at the moment: stay in her room patting her back until she drifts off, rock or feed until he falls asleep, etc. I have a friend who drove around in her car until her son fell asleep in his car seat, and then transferred him to his crib. Another friend took this a step further by parking the car in the garage and then sleeping there herself, fearing she would wake the finally sleeping child! These are all commonly used strategies for handling the tough bedtime challenge.

WHY STAYING WITH YOUR BABY HAS LONG-TERM CONSEQUENCES

Although this short-term choice may seem like a great option at the time, it's just not that easy because it comes at a substantial cost.

Interferes with your baby's development of self-reliance. Staying with your baby until he or she falls to sleep creates a lasting dependence. What you're actually teaching your child is that she can only fall asleep *as long as you are there.* This goes against what we know about the importance for children of learning to master valued tasks on their own. This strategy also deprives her of the opportunity to learn how to fall asleep on her own, making your child over reliant on you and under reliant on herself. In other words, you are giving your child a fish, instead of teaching her how to fish. Similarly, teaching your child to rely on a bottle or pacifier to go to sleep is not teaching the skills needed for sleeping, because you (or, if you are lucky, your partner) *must* necessarily provide some assistance (e.g., finding the pacifier, refilling a bottle).

Once a baby learns that he needs your presence in order to get to sleep, it is not something he will easily outgrow or give up. So while you may be willing to rock an infant to sleep, you may be much less interested in staying in your toddler's room each night as she nods off (particularly if you also have a new infant who needs rocking!). This approach, not surprisingly, maintains a child's dependence on you over a long period of time—which isn't good for either of you.

Inconvenient and uncomfortable for mom and dad. Although there's not much about being a parent that is truly convenient, opting to stay with your child until he or she goes to sleep makes a tough job even tougher. At the very least, it's pretty boring to sit in a dark room waiting for your child to go to sleep. I can think of, oh, seventeen things I'd rather be doing at that moment, including cleaning the kitchen, talking with my husband, reading the newspaper, and even watching television. Moreover, after you rock—or feed or pat—your child until he or she is completely asleep in your arms, you are likely to wake him or her during the eventual transfer to the crib. Similarly, children who often appear to be sound asleep seem to have an uncanny ability to detect our attempted departure. Each of us has at times experienced the agony of defeat, when, after laying motionless for what seems like an eternity you shift out of bed and start to crawl across the dark room, hoping you don't land on a noisy toy. Just as you reach the door, you hear the dreaded cry and the process starts again from the beginning.

Even if you do successfully leave the room, what will happen when your baby wakes up in the middle of the night and realizes that you are not there? Guaranteed you will then need to return and be with them until they fall back asleep. Perhaps you can convince yourself at 8 or 9 PM that rocking or patting your baby for fifteen or twenty minutes while he or she falls asleep is relaxing "quality time." You will probably not have the same reaction at 3 AM. In sum, making this short-term choice about getting your baby to sleep can lead to long-term consequences for you and your baby.

WHY PUTTING YOUR BABY TO BED WITH A BOTTLE OR PACIFIER HAS LONG-TERM CONSEQUENCES

Although the short-term choice of giving your baby a pacifier or bottle to help him fall asleep (more on this in Chapter 4) may appear to avoid some of the inconvenience of staying with your child until he falls asleep, it too has long-term consequences:

Interferes with your baby's development of self-reliance. Remember that this choice requires the use of a mechanical device—meaning something that can, and will—be lost in a dark room. A baby who can't locate a pacifier will cry out for a parent to come and find this object. A child who finishes his bottle of milk or water at night will cry out for a new bottle. And you will have to come and locate the object, or pour a new bottle, to help your baby get back to sleep.

Causes health problems. As I briefly mentioned in the breast-feeding chapter, babies who go to sleep sucking on a bottle are significantly more likely to suffer from various health problems, including ear infections, tooth decay, asthma, wheezing, allergies, and obesity. The reason for this is simple: when a child falls asleep while drinking from a bottle, milk pools in the mouth and remains there virtually all night, which in turn leads to tooth discoloration and decay. Drinking while lying down also increases a child's risk of ear infections. The milk drips into the eustachian tube of the middle ear, causing irritation which leads to ear infections. This is a great example of the long-term consequences of making short-term choices: The price for taking this short-cut is an ear infection and/or asthma that both require considerable time and attention.

Leads children to associate food with sleep. Another problem with giving your baby a bottle in bed is that it ultimately leads the child to associate falling asleep with eating. Children who develop a connection between feeling very full (or actually eating and/or drinking) while they are drifting off to sleep, will come to rely on this strategy later in life. They may insist on a large bedtime snack or want to eat just prior to going to bed, which can have serious consequences in terms of obesity. Given what we now know about the growing epidemic of obesity and its very serious health consequences (more on this in Chapter 5), think very carefully about whether you really want to create a link between sleeping with eating and/or drinking.

Leads to toilet training problems. A large quantity of liquid (in a cup or bottle) at bedtime can lead to problems with toilet training. Because what goes in must come out, children who drink to get to sleep are particularly likely to have problems with bedwetting. So you may experience challenges later on as you start to face toilet training.

"FERBERIZING"

Probably the most famous approach to getting your child to sleep is the Ferber method. Dr. Richard Ferber is a sleep specialist at Harvard University, and his approach has received a lot of attention in the media (including a fictional demonstration in the 1990s on the sitcom *Mad About You*). In brief, "Ferberizing" your child involves letting them cry it out. You put them in their bed, you reassure them that everything will be fine, and you leave. If they cry, you wait a certain amount of time (maybe five minutes at the beginning, but the time gradually increases to ten, fifteen, twenty minutes and more), then return and briefly comfort them. Then you leave again and they cry again. This pattern—child cries, parent waits, parent returns, parent leaves—is repeated until the child stops crying.

Does this approach work? Well, to paraphrase ex-President Bill Clinton, it depends on what "works" means. Everyone who tries this approach agrees that there is some initial period of days or weeks that is very unpleasant.

Basically you sit and listen to your child sob hysterically. Over time, the child learns that you are not returning and stops crying, and hence the approach "works." In this sense, the Ferber method can be seen as an effective approach to getting your child to go to sleep on his or her own. But this approach is really just another short-term choice with long-term consequences for you and your baby.

WHY "FERBERIZING" HAS LONG-TERM CONSEQUENCES

Although the Ferber approach to getting your baby to sleep may seem like a good idea, particularly for sleep deprived parents who are willing to try anything in hopes of getting a good night's sleep, this approach has two major long-term consequences:

Disrupts your baby's development of attachment. The main problem with the Ferber method from the slow and steady perspective is that it disrupts the crucial parent-child attachment bond. Instead of reinforcing in your child their ability to depend on you at a time of need, they learn that you are not there when they need you. Over time, children—and even infants—placed in this situation will stop calling—or crying—for you. But the problem is really *why* the child stops crying, namely because he has learned his cries are useless, because they will not give him what he truly needs, in this case the comfort and reassurance of a caretaker. Is this the message you want to send your child? My feeling is that the cost of fostering self-reliance in this way is just too high a price to pay for both you and your baby.

Creates emotional distress for mom and dad. Even parents who are desperate for a good night's sleep find listening to their baby cry difficult—and this is a very necessary part of the Ferberizing approach. Even parents who have "successfully" used this approach to getting their child to sleep describe this part of the process as very draining. I cannot stomach this approach because I find it upsetting and difficult to hear my child cry for an extended period of time.

WHY THE SLOW AND STEADY APPROACH TO BEDTIME HAS LONG-TERM ADVANTAGES

My slow and steady approach to the challenge of sleep focuses on using this challenge as an opportunity to help you and your baby. The advantages of this approach are:

Develops self-reliance. It's our responsibility to help our kids develop the skills needed for getting to sleep on their own because sleep is necessary to functioning well in life. Although we may be tempted to think of sleeping as a very simple task for a child, many children actually need to be taught specific skills to allow themselves go to sleep. After all, few adults simply crawl into bed and immediately go to sleep—many of us go through elaborate rituals. We may read or watch TV, or—at least before we have children—have sex. We use various activities to help ourselves get to sleep, so why should we place our children in a sterile environment and expect them to magically fall asleep on their own?

Enhances the parent-child attachment bond. By returning to your baby's room periodically while he or she is falling to sleep you are demonstrating your availability and concern, but aren't teaching your baby to rely on your physical presence to fall asleep.

THE SLOW AND STEADY APPROACH TO HELPING YOUR BABY (AND YOU) SLEEP

Here's how you can get your child to sleep without creating excessive dependence or disrupting the attachment bond:

1. Create a distinct bedtime routine.

One way children feel in control of their worlds—as we adults do—is with a schedule. Even before they can tell time, they know that bedtime regularly comes after other activities, such as dinner, story time, and a bath. Setting up a distinct bedtime routine that you follow every night is therefore one effective way of helping children get themselves to sleep. In my family, this routine involved reading a book and then turning on a CD of classical music. Other parents might want to incorporate other calming rituals, such as singing a lullaby, saying prayers, or telling a story. It doesn't matter which particular routine works best for your family, as long as that routine is generally followed each time your child is going to sleep.

However, this routine needs to be relatively brief—ideally in the ten- to fifteen-minute range. Children are very clever at trying to spend more time with their parents, particularly when they are trying to delay the start of bedtime, so make sure that your bedtime routine is "short and sweet."

2. Provide a clear transition from playtime to bedtime.

Toddlers especially need a chance to prepare themselves for sleep—which typically includes stopping some other fun activity in order to make the transition from playtime to bedtime much smoother. I use the kitchen timer—I give my children a warning that I am setting the timer for five minutes and then when the timer rings, they understand that it is time for bed.

3. Give toddlers opportunities to exercise choices regarding bedtime.

Children like control and predictability in their worlds, and providing opportunities for such control enhances their feelings of independence and autonomy. You can enhance your child's feelings of autonomy by offering choices that let him or her express specific preferences. For example, you could announce that in the twenty minutes before bedtime you could work with your child on a puzzle or play a game of Candyland. If you always read a bedtime story, you could offer your child two or three or four different book choices to hear. If your child always listens to music while going to sleep, you could offer a number of different tapes or CDs to choose from. All of these options help your child feel that some of the choices surrounding bedtime are his or her own—even if the ultimate choice of when and whether to go to bed is not!

4. Provide a comfort object.

Many children naturally form an attachment to a particular blanket, stuffed animal, or doll, which can all work well as a comfort object. Make sure the object is large enough not to be easily lost and can be found without adult help during the night.

5. Provide a crib activity.

Like adults, children benefit from performing special activities to help them make their transition to sleep. For infants, this can mean activities in the crib. One of my favorites is a Fisher-Price activity board that attaches to the side of the crib and has various interesting dials and buttons that even infants as young as five months can operate. Soft books are another good choice for an infant's crib. Toddlers benefit from having interesting toys like stuffed animals, dolls, and books. (Note that television and videos are not on this list—media exposure typically excites and arouses children, and hence does not help calm them for sleep. I'll discuss this in more detail in Chapter 8).

Both infants and toddlers can benefit from listening to music, ideally from a tape or CD, as they fall asleep. You can buy one of the specially-designed lullabies or nighttime music for children compilations, but any kind of quiet music, such as soft guitar or slow classical music, can work well. Music is calming for children and can also serve—particularly for younger children—as a clear signal that it is time for sleep.

6. Leave the room while the child is awake.

After the routine is finished you should leave the child's room, telling the child that you love them and will return later to check on them. Although it can be tempting to try to transition an infant from a sleeping position in your arms directly to a crib, this approach does not help the baby learn to put him or herself to sleep. For toddlers and preschoolers, you may want to suggest some things they can try to help themselves go to sleep. If they claim to not feel tired suggest they find a way to entertain themselves. Even a young child may enjoy looking at books alone, watching stars out the window, or thinking about fun things they did that day. Suggest specific strategies they can use to help themselves drift to sleep.

7. Return often to your child's room to provide reassurance, whether they call for you or not.

Return to your child's room *before* calling or crying out begins, even if that means you go back in thirty seconds. If you wait to return until a child is crying or calling for you, you are sending them the very clear message that these calls and cries will lead to your return, and thereby motivating these behaviors. My four-year-old son was perfectly willing to be alone in his room but wanted to know that people would check in on him from time to time. I promised to return every ten minutes until he fell asleep. Sometimes I would need to check two or three times before I found a sleeping boy, but many times he would not even be awake at my first check. Just knowing that I would return was enough to let him stay quietly in his bed. If you return to your child's room periodically while he or she is going to sleep, you are showing your child that you are available and concerned, but aren't teaching your child to rely on your physical presence to fall asleep.

8. Provide brief and boring comfort—don't linger.

The point here is not to provide an incentive for your child to stay awake, so don't be tempted to read or tell another story, pick them up or cuddle them. All you'll succeed in doing is to set up a reward system for staying awake, not for sleeping! Instead, the long-term approach lets your baby know you are there for them if they should need you, but not to motivate them to stay up for your exciting return. Your goal is to let your child know that you believe he is able to go to sleep on his own.

9. Help your baby get back to sleep quickly.

When children awake at night, as they all will at some point, you face an additional challenge: Getting your child back to sleep when you are probably mostly asleep yourself. For young infants, a nighttime wake-up is probably caused by hunger. Breast-fed babies in particular are likely to need a nighttime feeding (or two) for several months. This feeding should be done quickly and quietly so that you don't provide unnecessary stimulation and excitment. Try to keep the lights off or at least dim and to talk in a soft, gentle voice, if at all. When older children wake up at night, it is often due to a full bladder (for those who are toilet trained) or a scary dream. You should, in both cases, take care of the immediate need quickly and quietly, and then encourage the child to return alone to bed. You may have to repeat some of the steps described previously, such as turning on music that is associated with bedtime, tucking in a comfort object, and/or singing a lullaby. Just remember to stick with the regular nighttime routine to remind your baby that it is still time for sleeping.

Chapter 3
The Great Thumb-Sucking
versus Pacifier Debate

There are two camps of parents when it comes to pacifiers—the ones who use them, and the ones who won't let a pacifier within a mile of their child. Although I don't know why this issue is one that many people feel so strongly about, let me go on record as saying that pacifier use is not a philosophical issue with me—they just aren't the answer to *any* childcare problem.

YOUR BABY NEEDS TO SUCK

Babies from birth to about six months have a strong and innate need to suck. They find sucking anything—a bottle, a breast, a pacifier, their fingers, their toes, etc.—extremely gratifying. Moreover, because babies only learn how to control their hands well enough to rely on their own fingers or thumbs for sucking later on (typically between four to six months), they need assistance from their caregivers in finding a way to satisfy their intense sucking needs. Pacifiers do work in the short-term to soothe infants who are very sad because sucking is a major way that young children get comfort. (Pacifiers clearly got their name for a reason).

WHY USING A PACIFIER
IS VERY APPEALING . . .
PARTICULARLY IN PUBLIC SETTINGS

The reliance on pacifiers may be especially tempting in public situations when a screaming child could be embarrassing. We've all experienced a moment (and probably many moments) when the baby is screaming its head off in public, and at that precise moment we would give anything, and I mean anything, to have the child stop crying. Just think about the many times you've seen a parent in a public place "calming" their baby or toddler by plugging its mouth with a pacifier. The other popular time to offer an infant a pacifier is at bedtime as a way of helping them fall to sleep—or, even more importantly, to get them back to sleep when they wake up at 2 AM (and 4 AM and 6 AM). Sleep deprived parents are eager to try virtually anything to help their child go to sleep, and pacifiers, because they allow babies to fulfill their intense need to suck, can indeed work like a charm.

WHY USING PACIFIERS HAS LONG-TERM CONSEQUENCES

But while using a pacifier may seem like a convenient solution, it can lead to *significant* long-term consequences.

Pacifiers are inconvenient and unnatural. Although pacifiers can sooth a child, you have to have a pacifier to use it. And pacifiers have a way of disappearing—just ask your friends who use them. Pacifiers get dropped (and left) on the ground, lost in public places, and misplaced behind pieces of furniture and under car seats. You may not relish continually buying pacifiers or having multiple backup pacifiers with you at all times. But most importantly, there are very comforting natural ways for young children to satisfy their sucking needs that don't require any hardware—their thumbs and fingers!

Pacifiers don't help us understand why the child needs to be comforted. One of the main problems with using pacifiers is that relying on them to comfort a child often leads us to ignore the underlying problem. If you don't believe me, just watch the next time you are in a public setting with infants, and see what happens when a child starts to cry. Parents who rely on pacifiers typically locate a pacifier as quickly as possible and place it in the child's mouth. They don't ask the child how they are feeling or what has happened, and they don't first attempt to try other solutions (e.g., rocking the child, singing to the child, feeding or changing the child, etc.). Kids cry when something is wrong. It is their way of communicating, so if pacifiers are used to comfort children who are sad, to distract children who are angry, and even to entertain children when they are bored, you are missing the point; pacifiers are just not the answer to childhood boredom, anger, or inability to get to sleep.

Parents who don't rely on the quick-fix pacifier solution, on the other hand, will be highly motivated to figure out what is wrong when their child is upset, and try to respond to that particular need directly. A child who is lonely or scared, for example, may benefit most from being held or cuddled, whereas a child who is hungry needs to be fed. This type of responsive parenting is crucial to developing secure attachments—in fact, infants who are attached to their pacifiers are less likely to form secure attachments with their mothers compared to those who show an attachment to a blanket or other soft object. Using a pacifier therefore shortchanges your children by depriving them of a caregiver who is attuned and responsive to their distinct need at the moment. When we choose to use a pacifier instead of taking the time to address our child's specific needs, we shortchange ourselves as well.

Pacifiers create dependence on this particular method of self-soothing. It is very easy to start relying on using pacifiers in a variety of situations because they work well as a quick-fix. Often the initial desire to use pacifiers only at bedtime, for example, gives way to using pacifiers when a child is sick or sad, scared or tired, turning the pacifier into a parenting crutch. Parents who rely on pacifiers to comfort a fussy child when they want to finish a phone call, need a child to be quiet during religious services or at the grocery store, or are too tired to read a story at night to help a child fall asleep, are not tending to the child's needs. As parents we need to parent, not simply search for the kids' "off switch." Constant use of a pacifier teaches a child that sucking on an object is required to feel calm—which, over time, can lead a child to develop an intense psychological dependence on the object. This dependence on a pacifier for gaining comfort is similar to the dependence smokers feel with cigarettes—they can't imagine feeling relaxed and calm without a cigarette in their hand.

Pacifiers foster dependent behavior. The child who uses a pacifier does not get to control his or her own sucking needs. In fact, one of the things parents who use pacifiers like best is their ability to control the use of the sucking object by taking it away or restricting its use to particular times. An infant who cannot find the pacifier in a dark crib in the middle of the night must call out to you to locate it. This action of providing a child with a tool of comfort is a tool that the parent *must* provide. This short-term solution sets up a feeling of dependence, not at all the feeling of independence and self-soothing a child needs to succeed later in life. A pacifier robs a child of a sense of independence and control over their world.

Pacifiers interfere with breast-feeding. Sucking from a pacifier is very different from sucking from a breast. Breast-feeding requires vigorous sucking to extract milk, which can be undermined by the use of pacifiers, which require only gentle sucking. Babies who are learning to suck from a pacifier at the same time they are learning to suck from their mother's breast may develop nipple confusion. Latching on to a pacifier, which has a narrow base, is easier than latching on to the breast, which has a larger base.

Infants who use pacifiers may also satisfy their sucking needs in this way, and may therefore reject bottles and breasts, causing decreased frequency and duration of breast-feeding, which in turn is associated with numerous health problems (as described in Chapter 2). It is not surprising that babies who use pacifiers tend to be weaned earlier than those who are breast-fed.

Pacifiers create ear infections. Infants who use pacifiers are more than twice as likely to develop ear infections as those who don't. In fact, pacifier use alone is responsible for 25 percent of the ear infections that occur in children younger than three. Is it just prolonged sucking in general that leads to such problems? No—there is no association between thumb-sucking and ear infections or between breast-feeding and ear infections, suggesting that something unique about pacifiers leads to ear infections.

Pacifiers create dental problems. Pacifier use is also associated with various and lasting dental problems. Children who use pacifiers show alterations in the structure of the mouth and the position of the teeth, including the development of crossbite, as well as an increased risk of developing cavities. These changes to the structure of the mouth and teeth remain even after pacifier use is stopped.

Pacifiers create a parent-child power struggle. Don't ever think pacifiers are easier to control than thumbs—just ask the parent of a toddler or preschooler how easily their child gave up the use of their treasured "binkie"—it is rarely an easy process. Because we can ultimately take control of the pacifier—including controlling its availability and even restricting it completely—children often rebel against our effort to take control. Imagine if you were strongly attached to an object, and then someone suddenly took it away—you probably wouldn't react well. Similarly, although parents of children who use pacifiers often describe the benefits of being able to take away the pacifier, it is rare to find a parent who actually managed to take away a child's pacifier before he or she was ready to give it up without a substantial struggle. And how many teenagers do you know who suck their thumbs? In other words, why create a struggle over pacifier use at all—just say "no" to pacifier use from the beginning and eliminate this whole battle.

WHY THUMB-SUCKING HAS LONG-TERM ADVANTAGES

Although the age-old debate of thumbs versus pacifiers continues, nature has provided an obvious solution to this dilemma—thumb-sucking provides a way for every baby to satisfy their sucking needs without the long-term damaging effects of a pacifier on a child's body, mouth, and psyche. Thumb-sucking is a great solution for satisfying an infant's sucking needs for a variety of reasons—and also has many long-term advantages.

Thumb-sucking is a natural and healthy way of comforting one's self. The desire to suck one's own thumb and fingers is normal—fetuses suck in utero, and even very new infants try to bring their fingers and hands to their mouths. Why would you want to interrupt or interfere with such a natural impulse?

Thumb-sucking gives children the ability to comfort themselves at will. This is one of the ways that even very young babies can take care of their own needs, and hence gives them an important sense of independence. A thumb is always available, and entirely under the owner's control. And in turn, sleep deprived parents benefit because a child who wakes up at 3 AM is immediately able to find their own thumb and get back to sleep.

Thumb-sucking promotes independent thinking and requires the child to make choices. Because thumb-sucking requires "giving up" one of the child's hands, it imposes costs on a child that pacifier use does not. Very young babies naturally want to grasp objects, and will take their hands out of their mouths to do so. Hold a ball or truck or doll in front of a six month-old, and the hands or thumb quickly come out of the mouth as they grasp the desired object. Older babies who are eager to crawl need to use both hands to get around, which means they can't simultaneously suck their thumbs. Even children who suck their thumbs frequently are highly motivated to crawl, and stop sucking in order to perform these tasks. Similarly, older children who are interested in doing puzzles or painting on an easel or throwing balls face a similar choice—if they want to participate in these interesting activities, they simply must remove a thumb from a mouth because they need to use both hands. Because these activities are intrinsically interesting and appealing to infants and small children, they are highly motivated to use their hands in these situations. So, you should disregard any horror stories from friends about a child who sucked his or her thumb until fifth grade because their parents couldn't take it away like they could a pacifier.

Thumb-sucking can be more easily dropped as a habit. Because pacifier use doesn't interfere with other desirable activities, it is less likely to be naturally dropped as a habit. Children are perfectly able to crawl, walk, do puzzles, paint, and throw balls with a pacifier in their mouths—and they often do. I remember seeing numerous children in preschools and playgroups who were participating in a variety of activities, all while they had pacifiers in their mouths—the perfect example of a short-term fix that leads to a *very long-term problem*!

THE SLOW AND STEADY APPROACH TO SATISFYING YOUR BABY'S SUCKING NEEDS

So, what if you've now made a decision to avoid pacifiers, and to instead rely on thumb-sucking to fulfill your baby's sucking needs? Here's how to do it:

1. Give a very young infant your finger to suck.

Because very small infants lack the ability to move their own hands to their mouths on a consistent basis, or the strength to even hold their hands in a single place, they do need some assistance in finding ways to fulfill their intense need to suck. One way of providing sucking to infants is to breast-feed—as described in Chapter 2. If you are not breast-feeding or your child is not hungry, but needs extra comforting, you can offer your own fingers (after a careful washing, of course) for babies to suck on until they have the physical dexterity to reliably bring their own thumbs and fingers to their mouths. Here's how it's done: Try inserting a finger into your baby's mouth with the tip of your finger against the roof and the fingernail side facing the tongue to avoid accidentally hurting the baby with a jagged fingernail. I remember riding in a car most of the way between Massachusetts and New Jersey in this position to soothe my older son when he was only a few weeks old!

2. Encourage older infants to suck their thumbs and/or fingers.

Encourage your child to suck on his or her thumb when he or she is physically able to do so, by around age three to four months. Although you may initially have to help your baby find his thumb, he'll soon gain in physical dexterity and be able to find it on his own. When my kids would cry, I'd rock them and murmur "find your thumb, find your thumb," which they eventually mastered. Teaching your child to use his or her own finger or thumb for self-soothing takes a little bit of work, but is a great way of providing your child with an important tool for comforting him or herself.

3. Learn a variety of skills for comforting your baby.

Practice using a variety of different approaches for comforting your baby so that you, and your baby, learn together what strategies work best in different situations. Many babies who are tired or upset benefit simply from being held or rocked. Others find singing soothing (I remember singing verse after verse of "My Bonnie Lies Over the Ocean" to my older son whenever he was sad). Sure, these techniques are going to take more time and energy on your part than plugging your baby's mouth with a pacifier. But this type of responsive parenting involves working actively with a child to soothe tears, and fosters a secure parent-child attachment that will benefit you and your child for years to come.

4. Place limits on Thumb-Sucking for toddlers.

If you're worried that your kid is relying too much on thumb-sucking and you'd like to wean him or her off their thumb, you can start by placing limits or restrictions on thumb-sucking in a variety of ways. Both my sons sucked their thumbs from infancy (about three months or so) until the early toddler years (around age two). Neither of them sucked their thumbs at all by the time they were two-and-a-half-years old. How did I get them to stop sucking? Starting at around age two, any time they sucked their thumb, my husband and I referred to thumb-sucking as a sign they were tired, and announced our intention to let them go to their rooms to sleep as soon as possible. We wanted to send a very clear message that thumb-sucking by this age is a sign of being tired, and hence children who were sucking their thumbs needed to go to sleep. Usually this announcement met with great protest—and the immediate removal of the thumb from the mouth. Within a month or so of starting this plan, thumb-sucking stopped completely. It was an easy and painless solution that worked to the advantage of both parents and child.

5. Set and enforce strict limits on pacifier use.

If you find you must use a pacifier in the early months, restrict its use in numerous ways so that it does not become a crutch—for you or your child. First, rely on a pacifier only when your child is going to sleep, which is typically the time in which babies are most in need of intense sucking. Do not carry extra pacifiers in your purse or car to provide when your child is upset or sad, lonely, or bored. Second, make sure that providing a pacifier is the last approach you try to comfort your child. Using a pacifier should be a backup strategy for soothing your child after other strategies, such as rocking, singing, and holding, have all failed to comfort your child. Third, to minimize psychological dependence as well as the negative physical consequences, stop all pacifier use by the time your baby is about six-months-old. Infants younger than six-months-old use pacifiers to satisfy their sucking needs, and if your baby is unable or unwilling to suck his thumb, he or she may need additional sucking stimulation (particularly if not breast-fed). But by six months, babies are using pacifiers for comfort as opposed to sucking needs, and therefore their dependence on a pacifier for security should be transferred to another object (e.g., a special blanket, a favorite stuffed animal, a doll, etc.).

Part 2

THE SECOND YEAR

Chapter 4
Healthy Eating

If you had a nickel for every time you and your toddler argued about food, you would be able to retire at fifty. Most parents face these battles over food several times a week—or even several times a day. But here's the good news—by making long-term food choices, you can eliminate food fights altogether.

THE FIGHT OVER FOOD

Sure, I want my child to eat healthy foods—but in reality, this just isn't as easy as it seems.

First, children tend to gravitate towards the most unhealthy foods possible—white bread, sugary cereals, salty French fries, and all sorts of desserts (e.g., cookies, cakes, candies, etc.). Even if you know these aren't very nutritious foods, they can be very tempting to serve because you know your child will eat them.

Second, it's hard to find time to sleep, let alone shop and cook and wash dishes. And unfortunately, unhealthy foods, such as those found in drive-in restaurants and prepackaged lunches, are often faster and more convenient to obtain than healthy ones, like fruits and vegetables. It's very easy to pick up unhealthy foods, like hamburgers, French fries, and sodas, without even leaving your car. It's considerably harder to pick up healthy foods in a drive-through—even when a fast food restaurant advertises salads or other healthy fare, these foods are often covered with high fat dressing.

These two factors lead parents to make quick-fix food choices, such as fast foods and foods high in fat and sugar, instead of long-term food choices—home-cooked meals that include and fruits and vegetables.

WHY BAD EATING HABITS HAVE LONG-TERM CONSEQUENCES

Despite the appeal of easy and unhealthy short-term food choices, they jeopardize the future health of you and your baby. Unhealthy eating in childhood:

Creates lifetime food preferences. One of the major problems with giving your kids unhealthy foods is that these early experiences with food have a lasting impact on what they prefer to eat—this is one reason why children who grow up in different cultures have very different taste preferences later in life. So, if your child's earliest taste experiences include lots of fat, sugar, and salt, these are the tastes he or she will quickly grow to prefer. If you eat highly processed white bread as a young child, you then prefer this type of bread to healthier wheat bread later on. Similarly, if you always add butter to a child's pasta, or sugar to cereal, the child will become used to this taste and will reject foods served without added fat and or sugar.

Creates obesity. As we continually hear from the leading health experts, America is truly experiencing an epidemic of obesity—estimates suggest that 50 percent of Americans are overweight, and 11 percent of American children ages six to seventeen are obese. Moreover, children who are obese as babies are much more likely to be obese later in life, in part because they develop a set number of fat cells during childhood and adolescence that will never disappear—they can only get bigger or smaller.

Causes dental problems. Refined sugar, such as that found in many desserts and even fruit juice, causes tooth decay, which can lead to cavities over time. The issue of tooth decay is particularly problematic for toddlers, whose teeth brushing habits often leave much to be desired.

Enhances desire of rewarded food. Even parents who generally provide healthy and nutritious foods for their children, may choose to use unhealthy foods as a reward for engaging in particular desirable behaviors. If you are like most parents, you've relied on precisely this strategy because it seems to work. How many times have you heard a parent (or yourself) offering a child a food reward for some type of good behavior (e.g., cleaning their room, sitting quietly during church, or being good in the grocery store)? Ironically, one of the most common ways we parents get our children to eat healthy foods is by offering unhealthy foods as a reward! One study of parents of preschool children found that 56 percent reported promising children a special food, such as a dessert, for finishing another food, such as vegetables.

Unfortunately, providing an unhealthy food as a reward for eating a healthy food simply makes the unhealthy food appear especially appealing, and the healthy food particularly undesirable. The message you are sending if you insist that your child finishes his or her dinner before having dessert is basically that dinner is eaten only because it allows you to enjoy the desirable food, and not because the dinner itself is an enjoyable experience.

Moreover, children figure out very quickly that the "good foods" come after the "bad foods," and in fact, show an increased desire for "forbidden" foods. In one study three- to six-year-old children were sometimes allowed to eat a variety of different types of fruit cookie bars, and at other times were specifically told they could eat a fruit cookie bar they wanted except for one particular flavor (such as apple or peach). Researchers then measured how much children talked about each of the kinds of cookie bars, how much they tried to obtain them, and how much they asked for them. There were no real differences between interest in the different types of fruit cookie bars when children could eat whichever flavor they wanted, but as soon as one type of cookie bar was forbidden, that food became very desirable!

WHY DEVELOPING HEALTHY EATING HABITS HAS LONG-TERM ADVANTAGES

A long-term approach to healthy eating is based in the belief that children need to learn to prefer healthy foods over unhealthy ones, and it is your responsibility to help them develop such preferences by providing healthy foods while allowing them to make their own food choices. Here's what's so good about taking a long-term approach to food:

Creates healthy lifetime eating habits. Exposing your child to healthy foods during his or her early months and years helps them develop a preference for these types of tastes. If you offer your toddler whole wheat bread, fresh fruits and vegetables, and low-fat cheese and yogurt, he or she will naturally develop a preference for these types of healthy foods. When my children come home from school and want a snack, they invariably ask for healthy foods— hummus and carrots, apples and strawberries, and low-fat yogurt and cheese sticks. They only eat wheat bread, and they almost always drink water or skim milk (or calcium-fortified orange juice on occasion). This is not because I've refused to give them other foods, but simply because we don't have them in the house, and hence I don't offer them, nor are they in the habit of eating or requesting such foods. Similarly, both of my sons grew up eating waffles and pancakes using yogurt or applesauce (as opposed to sugary syrup) as a topping. When they (eventually) noticed that their father and I were using something else as a topping on our food, we simply explained that syrup was for adults—like coffee and beer! I've also added healthy foods to my sons' diets in subtle ways, such as calling wheat germ "treat," and I regularly ask them if they'd like "treat" on their yogurt. My children will sometimes eat the wheat germ off of their yogurt and then ask for more "treat!"

Children who grow up without exposure to a given taste, or with only limited exposure, may also fail to develop a preference for such a taste simply due to lack of experience. My children were not allowed to have any soda as children—we simply didn't offer it to them either at home or in restaurants. When my five-year-old son attended a friend's birthday party at a local skating rink and Sprite and Coke were the only beverages offered, I decided not to interrupt the celebration and make Andrew stand out, and instead waited to see what happened. He asked for the clear liquid, took one sip, and then came over to me and asked if I could get him some regular water because he didn't like the bubble water! This is a great example of how his early taste experiences led him to prefer water to sugary soda.

Provides numerous long-term health benefits. Helping your child develop a preference for healthy food obviously leads to numerous long-term health benefits including a lower risk of developing obesity and diabetes. People who eat large quantities of fruits, vegetables, and fiber are much less likely to develop colon and rectal cancer, perhaps in part because these foods work to quickly rid the body of cancer-causing fats. Similarly, people who eat foods that are low in cholesterol, such as fruits and vegetables, as well as foods that are high in fiber, are less likely to develop coronary heart disease.

Eliminates parent-child battles over food choices. A long-term approach to choosing healthy food is based in the belief that children need to exert their own independence in part by selecting the particular types of food they want to eat, and that you therefore need to help your children develop a preference for healthy foods. Instead of simply insisting that your child eat a particular food, which invariably sets up a parent-child struggle, children who naturally develop a preference for certain types of foods will generally make healthy choices on their own (without parental pressure and rewards). After all, although in the short-term you do exercise considerable control over the foods your children eat, you need to make sure that your children continue to make these choices on their own, even when you are not there to make them "follow the rules."

Allowing your child to make food choices independently also means occasionally forgiving poor food choices and accepting that sometimes kids choose unhealthy foods. Recognizing this not only eliminates parent-child struggles over foods, but also makes bad food choices less appealing to kids than if you completely forbid them. In fact, restricting certain types of food leads these foods to be even more desirable to children. It is OK if your child eats cake and ice cream at birthday parties, has a piece of pie at Thanksgiving, and enjoys a children's meal from a fast food restaurant at times. What you want to teach is moderation, not abstinence.

You can do this by discussing some of the reasons for avoiding certain foods, or at least large quantities of certain foods. When my child begged for more than two cookies, I'd describe why I thought having more could be a bad idea, namely that it could make him sick. I'd point out the stories we've read about children who over-ate and became sick (like in *Curious George and the Chocolate Factory*), and suggest that my recommendation was to not have more of a particular food because I loved him and didn't want him to feel bad. But ultimately I left the decision up to him, meaning that if he truly felt he needed to have three cookies, and was willing to take the risk of developing a stomach ache, I allowed him to do so. And he almost always chose to follow my advice to not eat the desired food. This is a great example of showing responsive parenting yet allowing children to develop self-reliance.

THE SLOW AND STEADY APPROACH TO HEALTHY EATING

How can you get your child to eat a healthy and balanced diet and avoid fighting over food? Try these eight easy steps if you are interested in adopting the slow and steady approach to healthy eating.

1. Breast-feed.

As I describe in detail in Chapter 2, children who are breast-fed tend to have better eating habits, and are much less likely to develop obesity, than those who are formula fed.

2. Offer your child healthy foods—and drinks.

Because children's life-long taste preferences are influenced by their earliest experiences with food, you need to provide healthy and natural foods to your children early on. Along with offering healthy foods, you also need to offer healthy drinks—which for young children are primarily water and milk. Although fruit juices can be offered, you need to make sure that children are drinking only limited quantities of juice (ideally not more than four to eight ounces daily, and even then diluted with water). Fruit juices, especially apple juice and grape juice, do not have high quantities of vitamins and therefore do not provide the much needed nutrition that drinking milk does. Because of its relatively high sugar content, fruit juice can also lead to tooth decay. Finally, children who drink large quantities of juice are often less interested in drinking milk.

3. Avoid using food as a reward.

No matter how tempting it is, try to avoid requiring your child to eat one type of food (e.g., a vegetable) before eating a more desirable type of food (e.g., a dessert).

4. Practice what you preach.

Children watch your behavior and form many of their attitudes towards food by watching what you do. In turn, if your child sees you drinking soda, eating potato chips, and enjoying large desserts, he or she will likely form positive attitudes towards these foods. It can also be difficult to avoid allowing your child to taste whatever you are eating, which again can lead to early exposure to a particular taste. On the other hand, children who see their parents eating fruits and vegetables, drinking milk and water, and selecting wheat bread, will be more likely to gravitate towards these foods. You therefore have a responsibility to not only keep healthy foods in the house and readily available, but also to model your own enjoyment of such foods.

5. Allow your child to make his or her own food choices.

Children exert their independence in part by choosing the foods they want—and do not want—to eat, and you need to understand that this is an important developmental stage. Once you've provided a range of food options, you should then allow your child to select from within these options. It doesn't matter if the foods your child chooses seem odd or nutritionally unbalanced because nutrition will balance out over the course of the day or week. So, allow your three-year-old to eat peanut butter and jelly sandwiches for breakfast, cereal for lunch, and yogurt and crackers for dinner. The classic children's book *Bread and Jam for Frances* describes how children may prefer a certain food for several days in a row, but then grow tired of this choice.

6. Trust that your child will eat when he or she is hungry.

Although many parents are concerned about whether their child is eating enough food, children eat when they are hungry—so, your job is to provide adequate types of healthy foods to sample, and then to trust that your kids will eat what they need. If you've offered peanut butter, eggs, cheese, and fruit and your child is not interested, take this as a sign that he or she is not hungry, not as a sign to serve cookies, potato chips, and sugary juice. And remember, children have much smaller stomachs—and appetites—than adults. So, your toddler may eat a quarter of a sandwich or a few strawberries and feel completely full, whereas we may view this amount of food as not adequate for normal growth.

If your child is small for his or her age and you are concerned about whether your child is eating enough, don't simply resort to providing foods you know your child will enjoy, such as sugary cereal, sweet juices, and overly processed foods. One of my friends had a four-year-old son who was quite small for his age, and hence, she would make him milkshakes (using actual ice cream) for breakfast! If you have genuine concerns about your child's size, talk to your pediatrician about whether your concerns are valid, and if so, how best to approach them. But don't rely on quick-fix solutions that may provide your child with adequate calories, but not appropriate nutrition.

7. Withstand peer pressure from others.

One of the hardest aspects of maintaining children's healthy eating is exposure to other children who are eating different types of foods. Many of us encounter strong pressure from our kids to buy the foods they see other children eating at daycare or advertised on television (yet another reason to turn off the TV—see point #8 below!). Or, let's not forget well-meaning family members who want to serve your children foods you'd rather they not have. Your mother, for example, may insist that having ice cream every day after dinner is exactly what you enjoyed as a child, and obviously that led to no long-term negative effects.

How can you withstand such pressure? One way is to try to avoid particular situations completely. Don't take your kid to McDonald's and expect him to order a salad! In other cases, you can simply explain to your children—and to any concerned bystanders—that your family follows certain rules about eating. When my sons were preschoolers, we spent a week in a beach house with another family whose three children were a few years older and had very different eating habits—their diets regularly included soda, potato chips, and ice cream! My older son certainly was aware of this difference, and asked if he could have some of what they were having. We said "no," and that our family had different rules about food.

8. Turn off the television.

As I'll discuss in detail in Chapter 6, one of the major factors contributing to obesity in children is exposure to numerous television advertisements that promote unhealthy foods. Children see an average of one food commercial every five minutes while watching television, and, as you might imagine, virtually all of these advertisements promote non-nutritious foods, such as fast food, sugary cereals, salty snack foods, and soda. This exposure can lead children to desire these foods, and to recognize them and ask for them in the grocery store. Avoiding television can thereby help reduce your child's recognition of and interest in various unhealthy food options.

Chapter 5
Television

For most toddlers—and even babies—growing up today, television and videos are just a natural part of the daily routine. And although allowing your child to watch television may seem like a harmless, and even inevitable, decision, this is not a choice you should make lightly. Exposing your kids to television can have a number of negative consequences and few, if any, advantages. The good news is that by "just saying no" to television, you and your child can learn to enjoy each other's company and that leads to both short- and long-term advantages.

WHY KIDS WATCH SO MUCH TV

Although the American Academy of Pediatrics recommends that children watch no more than one to two hours of television a day—and that those under the age of two watch no television at all—children ages two to five watch an average of twenty-eight hours of television each week, and on a typical day 59 percent of children under the age of two watch some television. Moreover, over 25 percent of children ages six months to two years have a television in their bedroom. In fact, the typical child spends more time watching television than doing anything else except sleeping!

Why do children watch so much TV? First, many parents rely on television as a convenient, free, and very effective babysitter—television does serve to hold children's attention, sometimes for amazingly long periods of time. Even young babies are often entranced by watching the moving lights and hearing the sound from the television screen, and will therefore "watch" television with rapt attention. Toddlers and preschoolers are typically more discriminating media viewers and are more likely to have particular preferences for television shows and videos. They often like to watch the same video or television program over and over again, just as they like to hear the same books read repeatedly. Given the appeal of television to children, many parents are very willing to turn on a child's favorite program or video, perhaps to help them settle down after a busy day at school, relax before bedtime, or reward them for good behavior. In fact, some parents can't even imagine how they could manage to cope without relying on their children's desire to watch television and its miraculous ability to hold their children's attention. Television is especially useful as an electronic babysitter when parents need to focus on various tasks, such as doing laundry, fixing dinner, or making phone calls.

Second, many parents see television and/or videos as having some type of educational value, and thus believe that their child is benefiting from such exposure. They describe how their children have learned letters, numbers, songs, and facts about the world from watching educational programs and videos. Even parents of very young infants sometimes show their babies videotapes that supposedly stimulate intellectual development. The line of *Baby Einstein* videos was created in the mid-1990s as a way to expose infants to poetry, language, music, and art, and parents may feel pressure to allow their child to benefit from such early exposure. This pressure is especially strong when it appears that all other infants are watching such tapes. Similarly, the television program *Teletubbies* was designed specifically to appeal to children under the age of two, and has been wildly successful.

Parents of preschool-age children may worry that their child will experience social difficulties if not exposed to popular television or video programs. After all, if the other children are talking about a favorite television character and their child isn't involved in the conversation, won't he or she feel excluded? Moreover, children's programs, such as *Sponge Bob Square Pants*, *Teletubbies,* and *Rugrats*, often feature merchandise tie-ins, such as toys and games. Parents may therefore feel it is unfair to deprive their children of the opportunity to watch popular television programs and videos, in part because they see such exposure as an important way of helping their children participate in social interactions.

WHY TELEVISION AND VIDEOS HAVE LONG-TERM CONSEQUENCES

So, you are probably already aware of the benefits of allowing your child to watch television and videos—but I bet you are much less aware of the considerable drawbacks to this decision.

Creates obesity. As you've probably heard, obesity among children is a considerable health problem in the United States today, with up to 15 percent of children ages six to eleven classified as obese. And children who watch a lot of television are more likely to be overweight than those who watch less television. A recent study in the *Journal of the American Medical Association* found that every two hours a day spent watching television leads to a 23 percent increase in obesity and a 14 percent increase in diabetes. What explains the link between television watching, obesity, and diabetes? Scientific evidence points to several potential explanations:

—Watching television is a passive activity (particularly with the advent of the remote control). So when your child sits in front of the television, he or she is not engaging in any type of physical activity. Moreover, while watching television the body's metabolic rate drops, meaning they are burning even fewer calories than they would while doing a puzzle, building with blocks, or even looking at books.

—Television viewing promotes poor eating habits, in part because watching television exposes your child to frequent advertisements for unhealthy foods. The average child sees more than 20,000 TV commercials in a year, and can you guess what the two most common types of advertisements are in shows targeting children? Toys and food. Food and eating references are presented nearly five times for every thirty minutes of primetime television programming (including commercials), and naturally these food advertisements aren't promoting the benefits of fresh apples, carrots, and wheat bread. One study of the types of food advertisements featured during Saturday morning cartoons revealed that two-thirds of the advertisements were promoting fats, oils, sweets, and high-sugar cereals. Given the prevalence of food-related advertising on television, it's not surprising that more than half of nine- to ten-year-old children believe that Ronald McDonald knows what is good for children to eat!

Models unhealthy behaviors. Both television and videos often feature characters smoking and drinking, which in turn can lead children to form positive images of both of these destructive behaviors. And this presentation of smoking and alcohol use as desirable occurs even in films targeted to very young children. One study in the *Journal of the American Medical Association* examined the presence of tobacco products (cigarettes, cigars, and pipes) in fifty G-rated animated children's films, including *Bambi*, *Lady and the Tramp*, and *The Lion King*. Tobacco use was portrayed in 56 percent of the films, including all seven films released in 1996 and 1997 (the latest years included in the study). Moreover, "good" characters are as likely to use tobacco as "bad" ones, and smoking in particular was often portrayed as glamorous and cool. Similarly, 50 percent of these films included alcohol use, and again, such use was just as likely to occur with good characters as bad characters.

Creates fear. Many children report seeing something on television or in videos that scares them. One study of college students found that 61 percent reported experiencing general anxiety after seeing something on television as a child, 46 percent experienced some type of wild imagination (e.g., monsters under the bed), 29 percent reported experiencing a specific type of fear (e.g., sharks, spiders, snakes), and more than 20 percent reported experiencing some type of sleep disturbance (e.g., nightmares, insomnia, need to sleep with lights on). The fear induced by mass media exposure is often long-lasting and quite intense. My husband, who grew up in Florida, remembers seeing the movie *Jaws* as a young child, and then developing an obviously irrational fear about swimming in the ocean. And this experience is sadly not uncommon— seeing upsetting events in the media changes children's willingness to engage in related behaviors. For example, children who watch a video showing a person drowning are less interested in going on a canoe trip, and children who watch a video showing a house fire are less eager to build a fire in a fireplace.

However, we are often unaware of our children's experience of fright reactions in response to media, in part because children may avoid mentioning such experiences. This underestimation of the frequency and intensity of children's fright reactions contributes to our willingness to allow our children to see television events that are intended for adults. Almost half of four-to-ten-year old children had seen the movies *Poltergeist* and *Jaws*, which were clearly intended for adult populations.

Increases levels of aggression. One of the most serious consequences for children who regularly watch television and videos today is their impact on levels of aggression—children who are exposed to violent media images engage in more aggressive behavior. The relationship between watching television and aggression is as strong as the link between smoking and cancer, and is particularly strong in boys. And unfortunately, watching violent television even impacts behavior later in life. For example, children who watch more violent television, such as *The Six Million Dollar Man, Starsky and Hutch,* and even *Road Runner* cartoons, behave more aggressively fifteen years later.

Why does watching violence on television or in movies lead to aggression? One reason is that this type of exposure teaches children appropriate ways to act, identify with television characters, and believe in the realism of television violence. Exposure to media violence can also increase levels of physiological arousal, which in turn can lead to aggressive behavior. Moreover, the link between watching television violence and aggression is circular, with television violence increasing aggression and aggression increasing attraction to television violence.

And even children who don't watch television that models physical aggression are very likely to see shows that model verbal aggression. Some of the most popular children's television programs today include inappropriate, and often rude, language. For example, the character

Angelica on *Rugrats* often sneers "Stupid babies" to other children, the term "You loser" is used with some regularity in the cartoon *Arthur*, and *Sponge Bob Square Pants* frequently utters "I hate you." These negative and aggressive terms are therefore learned and then repeated by children who watch these programs.

Decreases time spent in other activities. Perhaps most importantly, time spent watching television and videos takes time away from other activities that children can do on their own and with you. Children need to use their imaginations to learn to pretend, draw, build, be physically active, question, socialize, and cooperate. Television not only provides none of this but it also takes away valuable time in which children could be working on these valuable life skills. These negative effects of TV watching are particularly strong in children ages two to five.

Television viewing by young kids also leads to the formation of habits and preferences for watching television as opposed to other activities, meaning the effects of such viewing are long-term (not just time displacement). Not surprisingly, children who watch a lot of television in their early years watch a lot of television in later childhood and adolescence. I'm sure you've never heard any parent complain, "My child just doesn't watch enough TV." However, many parents complain that their children watch too much television. And they are right. I once called a friend of my son's and asked his father if he was available for a play date after school one day. The father called back later to say that he had managed to convince his son to go on the play date, but that it was very tough because he didn't want to miss his favorite TV programs to play with a friend!

If you are thinking about letting your child watch television, or if your child already watches television, ask yourself a simple question: What else would my child be doing in this time if he or she were not watching television? Chances are the answer is probably that it would be better for your child to be doing something else, like building with blocks, playing with dolls, drawing with crayons, riding a bicycle, or socializing with other kids. All of these activities help develop and foster long-term skills that watching television does not.

Impairs intellectual development. Although you might believe that at least some television programs have educational benefits, the truth is that there are simply no *proven* benefits of television watching on children's academic and/or intellectual development. Children who watch certain educational television programs may show some recognition of letters, numbers, and sounds, but this exposure does not lead to more general intellectual gains.

More importantly, neurological development, such as language and intellectual development, can't come from exposure to radio and television—children require active interaction with other humans to do this. Children may, for example, "learn" the alphabet on television, but this doesn't mean they understand what a letter is, or that is forms a word. In contrast, children who are watching television are failing to actively engage in and interact with their environment—all television programs, even those designed to be educational, represent a purely passive experience for children. As described eloquently by Marie Winn in her classic book *The Plug-In Drug*, "one is always *watching television* when one is watching television rather than having any other experience." Watching television is a one way street—by this I mean that there is no interaction to allow them to hear and model language. They are not able to ask questions or hear answers—which is precisely the way children learn language.

Shortens attention span. Many child psychologists note that even high quality programs such as *Sesame Street* lead to a shortened attention span simply because television creates an expectation of rapid change. I've heard many long-time elementary school teachers complain that children raised in an intensely media-focused environment expect similar excitement and rapid change during the school day, and can in turn lack the ability to focus consistently on less stimulating forms of education. Watching television and videos requires less concentration than reading or listening to music, which is one of the reasons why children find it so appealing. And you don't have to take my word for it—research demonstrates that for every hour of TV that a child between the ages of one and three watches, his chance of having an attention problem at age seven increases by nearly 10 percent. Researchers now believe that young children who watch two or more hours of television a day develop the "two-minute mind," meaning they have trouble concentrating on organizing information.

WHY CONTROLLING MEDIA EXPOSURE HAS LONG-TERM ADVANTAGES

The long-term approach to media exposure, in a nutshell, is as little as possible, as late as possible. The costs of television exposure, even in relatively small amounts of an hour or two a day, are considerable. Your long-term approach should provide your children both with true intellectual stimulation and give them the tools they need to entertain themselves.

Children need to interact with their environment to learn. If you want to foster your child's intellectual development, work with your children on puzzles, read to them, and answer their thousands of questions. But don't feel you need to spend all of your time playing with your children—simply interacting with your children as you go about your daily tasks provides numerous benefits that media exposure does not. Children can learn counting by helping measure cups of rice while you prepare dinner, work on hand-eye coordination by practicing sweeping the kitchen floor, or gain physical dexterity by trying to fold laundry. Involve your child in your normal daily activities—they learn skills and you get to spend *real* quality time sharing life experiences.

Children need to learn how to entertain themselves. The ability to find one's own entertainment is a crucial part of developing independence and self-reliance, and teaches children important life-long skills about creating their own entertainment to alleviate boredom (more on this in Chapter 7). So, if you make the tough choice to opt-out of the free and easy babysitting that television and videos provide, and instead try to interest your child in more active and stimulating forms of entertainment (e.g., doing puzzles, reading books, playing outside), you are providing your children with life-time benefits—greater physical activity and fitness, the opportunity to learn skills for entertaining themselves, and the development of greater curiosity and creativity.

THE SLOW AND STEADY APPROACH
TO AVOIDING TELEVISION ADDICTION

Although turning off the television may seem like an impossible task, it's not as difficult as it sounds—and as we've seen, the benefits are immense. So, here's how you can avoid falling into the trap of television and videos in this media-intensive age:

1. Avoid all videotapes.

The American Academy of Pediatrics advises that parents avoid all television viewing for children under the age of two. This age group needs direct interaction with caregivers to develop cognitively, not simply passive exposure to television and videos. It doesn't matter if it seems like everyone else is doing it—exposing an infant or small child to television in any form is simply a bad idea. This also includes videos such as *Baby Einstein* and *Mozart*, neither of which has the ability to make your child a genius, but as we've seen can have an adverse effect.

2. Develop non-media strategies for coping with boredom.

Develop other strategies for filling your kids' time so you don't fall into the trap of popping in a video when they complain that they're bored. This isn't as difficult as it seems—pick up copies of parenting magazines such as *Parents* and *Child*, for inspiration. They often contain new ideas for projects and activities in each issue. Keep a closet full of random objects that you might be tempted to throw away. Think back to when you were a kid to what kept you busy in the good old days before videos. It doesn't take much to create interesting projects for children. My own "children's closet" includes various art supplies (Playdough, markers, chalk), books of mazes and "connect the dots," stickers, beads, and bubbles. For young children, blowing bubbles and working with Playdough is often appealing enough. For older children, sorting buttons, drawing with crayons, or building with Legos, can be useful on a rainy day. And children of course have their own individual preferences about what they like to do best—for my older son, baking (especially cookies or brownies) always beats television, whereas for my younger son, playing hockey in the driveway is always his first choice.

3. Allow your children to experience boredom.

In today's busy society, many of us are focused on keeping our children constantly entertained and active. You've probably heard about two- and three-year-olds who participate in numerous scheduled activities each week, including ballet, gymnastics, art class, music class, and multiple play dates. But boredom is OK—and is even good. Children who are bored learn the valuable skill of developing creative strategies for coping with boredom. When my son is bored, he may work on digging a hole to the center of the earth, create a huge marble tower, or look at a book. These are all good uses of time because they force children to work creatively, imaginatively, and independently.

4. Read to your children.

One of the best long-term slow and steady parenting approaches is reading to your children. It requires intensive time and energy initially, but leads to rewarding long-term benefits. The intimacy reading requires fosters closeness between parent and child but it takes a lot of time and effort to read to your children, especially as kids get older and prefer longer and longer books. It can also be boring for the reader, particularly because children often want to hear the same book over and over and over again. My son has gone through stages lasting weeks at a time in which all he wants to hear is *Curious George Goes to the Hospital*, *The Mouse Family*, or *Sam and the Firefly*. (I have to admit that at one time, I hid *Sam and the Firefly* for a solid week simply because I could not bear to read it yet again). And reading naturally stimulates and enhances creativity, increases vocabulary, and improves imagination—all things that media exposure doesn't.

If you are bored reading the same old books, don't be afraid to go to your local bookstore or library and get some new ones. Even if your child is attached to a favorite few—kids adapt well and after initial resistance, will come to adopt new favorites. I found the best way to choose new titles is to consult *The New York Times Guide to the Best Children's Books*. It lists over 700 great books for children of various ages, and includes a plot summary of each so that you can choose those books that will best fit your child's particular interests. Feel free to "up the level" to give children a sense of challenge as well. When my older son was four, I read a series of classic books to him, including *Charlotte's Web*, *Stuart Little*, and *Little House in the Big Woods*. He was delighted with the longer stories, and looked forward to hearing what would happen to the characters the next night. Reading longer books also helps preschoolers work on memory and increases their vocabulary, and is hence a great preparation for kindergarten and beyond (unlike watching television).

5. Hire a babysitter when you need a break.

Many of us turn on the television or put in a video out of desperation—we simply need to make a phone call, cook dinner, or do some laundry. Another choice, however, would be to hire a neighborhood mother's helper to come and play with your child for an hour or so in the afternoon so that you could have time to complete such tasks. For only a few dollars (the cost of a cafe latte), you could have an hour of uninterrupted time while your child played with a high school student—who can introduce new games, supervise outdoor time, or play Chutes and Ladders. If finances are tight, see if you can propose a similar trade with a neighbor who also has young children.

6. Exercise control over media
   exposure—time, content, age.

If you have to rely on television or videos at times for whatever reason, choose what your children watch, when your children watch, and how much your children watch very carefully. Although no television program or video provides the benefits of true interpersonal interaction and independent exploration, some media choices are certainly better than others. To avoid exposing your children to unwanted advertisements, language, or social situations, select videos or public television over commercial television. Videos are also a better way of controlling the amount of television watched because they have a natural end—commercial television often goes quickly from one show to the next, which can make it more challenging to set limits.

When your child is watching a video or television, try to watch with them so that they are engaging in active social interaction as opposed to having an entirely passive experience. By sitting with your child during a program, you can answer their questions and engage them in a more interactive experience than if they are simply sitting passively watching television. My family even has a Friday night "movie night," in which we all sit together and watch a G-rated movie. You should also preview any video before showing it to your child to make sure it doesn't include acts of physical or verbal aggression, scary and/or inappropriate images, or modeling of tobacco and alcohol use.

Finally, try to choose videos that are lifelike and provide some information as opposed to those that simply provide entertainment. My older son watched no television or videos at all until he was five, at which point I bought a series of real-life activity videos that featured real people (not animation) and were instructional. For example, one video described the entire process of building a house, another described how food is made, and a third described airplane take-offs and landings. These videos were designed for children, but did not include fast changing scenes, animation, or other gimmicks. I also limited him (much to his regret) to a single video each afternoon, during his younger brother's nap.

7. Balance media with non-media time.

Because television watching is a passive and non-stimulating activity, make sure you are following up this activity with a more active and engaging form of entertainment. You could, for example, decide that after thirty minutes of television watching your child needs to have a very different type of activity, such as reading books, working on a puzzle, or playing basketball.

8. Keep the television off yourself.

As with all behaviors, children learn from watching their parents. And if you come downstairs to breakfast each morning and turn on CNN, or spend every Saturday afternoon watching sports, your children will quickly model that behavior. My husband and I watch television regularly (and probably far more television than we should), but virtually all of this television watching occurs after the children are in bed (e.g., between 9 PM and midnight). We also put our two televisions in "adult spaces" in the home, not children spaces—we have a television in our bedroom and in the living room, but not in the kitchen, the playroom, the family room, or the children's bedrooms.

Chapter 6
Independent
Play

Playtime is really "work time" for young kids—playtime fosters creativity and imagination, provides intellectual and physical stimulation, and gives much needed practice with social interactions. Playtime also provides a great opportunity for you to help your kids develop valuable life skills while simplifying your own life.

THE CHALLENGE OF KEEPING YOUR CHILD ENTERTAINED

One of the biggest surprises most parents of toddlers face is how very little our kids seem to be able to play on their own . . . and how very tiring it can be playing with a toddler. (This is one of the reasons many desperate parents turn to videos and television.) No matter how many toys and games you might have, your child will invariably be unable to find anything to play with unless someone else—ideally a parent—is constantly interacting with them. Although my husband used to pretend to play with our kids on Saturday mornings, they unfortunately became quickly dissatisfied with the "see how long Daddy can sleep on the couch" game. It's just easier to give in to the pleas and avoid the whining, fits, etc.—and provide constant entertainment. Those of us who work full-time may also feel a need to play with our kids constantly when we're home, in part to compensate for our absence. This focus on "quality time"—in lieu of quantity time—can mistakingly lead us to view entertaining our kids as a way to enhance the parent-child bond.

WHY ALWAYS ENTERTAINING YOUR KIDS HAS LONG-TERM CONSEQUENCES

You may think you are doing your kids a favor by spending long hours playing with them, but in reality this quick-fix solution has too many long-term costs for you and your kids.

Interferes with the development of independence and self-reliance. Kids who are constantly entertained by their parents or other adults don't have a chance to learn important skills for playing by themselves. This lack of self-reliance leads kids to be highly dependent on others for assistance—with completing a puzzle, building a Lincoln Log house, or drawing a picture on their own. After my husband spent several afternoons drawing with our younger son, Robert became unwilling to draw by himself because he saw his own drawing as inadequate— he then turned to an adult to draw "for him." Playing with your kids all the time therefore disrupts your child's ability to master the important life task of self-entertainment.

Interferes with the development of creativity. Kids who are constantly entertained never get the chance to create their own ways of playing, which inhibits their natural creativity and exploration. This inhibition manifests itself in very subtle ways. For example, even well-meaning parents unintentionally direct children in play—they may suggest objects for them to draw or build, demonstrate "the right" way of playing a game, or describe how a particular toy "should" be used. Parents also unwittingly evaluate children's play in various ways, which reinforces some types of playing and discourages others. We might, for example, give immense praise to a child who follows the directions exactly to build the Lego vehicle, but show less enthusiasm to a child who creates his or her own Lego creation. In line with this view, research suggests that kids who attend highly academic preschools—with a focus on teaching specific intellectual skills—are less creative as kindergartners, probably because they are responding to adults' directions instead of exploring on their own.

Exhausts parents. Let's be honest—a parent's job is tough enough with doing laundry, washing dishes, vacuuming—

we don't need to add playing with our kids for several hours a day to our already long "to do" list.

WHY INDEPENDENT PLAY IS GOOD FOR YOU AND YOUR CHILD

The long-term approach to play focuses on both encouraging children to play independently and, when you play with your child, following his or her lead. The advantages of this approach are numerous:

Fosters independence and self-esteem. Independent playtime lets kids feel good about themselves—because they choose the activity and control the rules—and gives kids a much needed chance to successfully accomplish something by themselves, any way they want. Remember, toddlers spend much of their lives being unable to do things on their own and following rules that others set up. Kids who can play by themselves also feel a great sense of pride because they have successfully mastered the valuable skill of being able to entertain one's self. Once my three-year-old, Robert, learned how to put together a puzzle by himself, he would sit for literally an hour working on very complex (sixty to one hundred piece) puzzles—and feel a great sense of accomplishment from completing them *by himself*. I was not surprised to hear from his preschool teacher that he was the only kid in his preschool class who refused help from teachers or peers with puzzles!

Enhances your child's intellectual development and creativity. One of the best ways to foster intellectual development is to let kids engage in independent exploration. Kids by nature are curious, and letting them choose activities to explore teaches them a lot about the world: What happens when a very large block is placed on a smaller one, how far will the ball go when I kick it like this, why won't the marble roll up-hill? Independent playtime also lets kids try out different roles and act out different feelings, without the influence or direction of parents or other adults. A child playing dress-up or with dolls, for example, may be exploring their concerns about an upcoming doctor visit or their excitement about attending a birthday party.

Simplifies parents' lives. Given our many other responsibilities as parents, we have limited time and energy to play with our kids, so it eases our lives when our kids can play at least sometimes by themselves. The long-term approach doesn't mean that you never play with your kids, just that you don't have to entertain them *all the time*. And frankly, we are better parents when we get a break sometimes!

THE SLOW AND STEADY APPROACH TO PLAY

Here's how you can teach your child to play independently and learn to play with your child in a responsive way:

1. Give a small number of specific play options.

Because young kids feel overwhelmed by having too many options, help your child select a play activity by asking them to select between only a few choices. For example, you might say, "Do you feel like working on puzzles, building with blocks, or looking at some books?" By helping kids focus on making a particular choice, you also encourage them to stay with that activity for a set amount of time, instead of quickly discarding it in favor of another activity. My kids' preschool, for example, asks kids to select one of four or five activity stations to play in each morning, which helps kids exercise independent choices—from a small number of options—and also maintain focus on a particular activity for some period of time.

2. Keep toy options exciting and new.

Children do get bored with playing with the same toys, so providing new toys on occasion helps to stimulate interest and excitement—and thereby encourage independent play. But this doesn't mean racing to the toy store every week. One approach is to rotate the toys your child currently has, so that only some of them are out at a given time. If you alternate toys monthly, even old toys that haven't been seen for a few weeks will seem new and exciting. Similarly, you can rotate books by making weekly trips to the library. Another strategy is to check out yard sales and flea markets, which often have great slightly-used toys at very low prices. And remember that many household objects can be great playthings for toddlers—pots and pans, measuring cups, egg cartoons, magazines and catalogs, toilet paper and paper towel rolls are all examples. Use your imagination, just think about how many times you've seen your baby ignore all of her toys in favor of your keys or eyeglasses.

3. Choose toys that enhance creativity.

Buy toys—such as blocks, Legos, dolls, dress-up clothes— that can be played with in many different ways, not just a single way. For example, one child might use blocks to build a garage for trucks, another might use them to create a dollhouse, and still another might use them to set up a farm. In contrast, if you get a toy that can only be used in one specific way, it becomes boring much faster—like many of the newer toys featuring lights, sounds, and batteries.

4. Check in frequently.

Kids can play alone for longer periods of time if they don't feel all alone. Checking in periodically lets them know you are there, and lets you give advice, praise, or direction if it is needed. Set your child up with an activity to get started on, and then check back in with him or her every few minutes. Over time, you can wait longer periods before returning as your child is more and more able to play independently.

5. Reward and praise independent play.

All kids—and adults—like rewards, so set up a specific reward system to reinforce your child's ability to play independently. I used to offer to read my children any book they chose after ten minutes of independent play, which was a great incentive for them. Kids also like praise, so make sure to let your child know you are proud of him or her for playing alone. Telling others—spouses, relatives, friends—about your child's ability to play alone is another good way of reinforcing this skill and encouraging future independent play.

6. Let your child take the lead when you play together.

When you do play with your kids, let them choose the activity and approach it in their own way, even if it is not the way the activity "should" be approached. For example, when you go on a walk with your kids, let them choose the pace and give them opportunities to explore whatever they'd like—puddles, leaves, bugs. Accept that sometimes their interests may seem odd to you or won't be what you expect. For example, many parents report taking their young children to the zoo—and watching them gravitate to the squirrels and pigeons. Similarly, I remember taking my kids to a fancy children's museum full of scientific exhibits that I was sure would entertain them for hours, and feeling great disappointment when all they wanted to do was ride the escalator. So step back, put your expectations aside, and let your kids explore the activity or environment in their own way—it's how they best learn about their very new world.

7. Describe, don't evaluate.

When your child asks what you think of something they've created, describe what you see instead of labeling or evaluating it. Avoid giving a name to the work of art or a block creation, which can lead your child to focus only on creating specific objects instead of engaging in more creative and open-ended exploration. Many adults try to identify a particular object when they look at kids' paintings when in reality, kids often paint simply to explore colors and textures, and not to create a literal representation of an object. Avoid giving an evaluation of the object, which can influence the direction of their future creations. Instead of saying "that's a very pretty picture," try saying, "I see reds and greens and blues, and some straight lines as well as curvy lines." This approach shows your child you are really responding to what he or she has created, but doesn't direct or control their future creative efforts.

8. Turn off the TV . . . and the computer.

As you now know (see Chapter 6), watching television doesn't help your child develop skills for playing independently—in fact, it leads kids to become dependent on external forms of entertainment. Similarly, avoid using the computer for entertainment—this is yet another passive approach to play that requires little imagination, provides little intellectual stimulation, and interferes with the development of independent play skills.

Part 3

THE THIRD YEAR

Chapter 7
Mastering Toilet
Training

Toilet training is an important developmental milestone—marking a child's first steps towards independence—and, like it or not, it is a task that the child controls. But if you take a long-term approach to toilet training you will help your child gain mastery, strengthen the attachment bond, and even simplify your life. If you are in the midst of this seemingly endless stage, read on: Once you understand the physical and psychological challenges of toileting training and follow a few simple rules, things will go much easier for you and your child.

WHY PARENTS WANT AN END TO DIAPERS

After two or three (or sometimes even more) years of changing diapers, it's no wonder some parents are desperate for their child to transition to underpants. It's hard to lift a thirty or forty pound child to a changing table, diapers and wipes are expensive, and it's embarrassing to hear stories from relatives or friends who report their eighteen-month-old is toilet trained when your nearly four-year-old refuses to use the potty on a regular basis. Moreover, on some level it's hard not to succumb to the erroneous conclusion that mastering toilet training is at least somewhat predictive of IQ. Before my three-year-old son started using the toilet, I hated hearing the stories from friends about their own children who regularly used the toilet. And I did wonder, like many of you who are no doubt in the same boat, whether Andrew's lack of interest in the toilet was a reflection of his limitations, or my poor parenting, or both.

It is factors like this that may lead us to push toilet training before our kids are truly physically and psychologically ready. You know what I mean—parents who buy potties for one-year-olds or encourage their eighteen-month-olds to sit on the potty, not to mention "educating" their children by buying many books and videos promoting the benefits of toilet training. These parents may also move their children from diapers to "pull-ups," a type of disposable diaper designed to look like underwear and can be pulled down and up like underpants so that a child can easily use the toilet—but unlike regular underwear, pull-ups are especially absorbent so that accidents do not soil clothes. Yet while you may be very eager for this transition, kids can be quite resistant to such change, which in turn sets up a classic parent-child battle. And this is a battle that the child will win every time.

SHORT-TERM APPROACHES TO TOILET TRAINING

Given parents' desperate desire to get their kids out of diapers, short-term approaches to toilet training often seem very appealing. Here are two of the most common quick-fix approaches:

Partial toilet training. This first approach involves aiming for "partial training" instead of complete toilet training. This approach focuses on getting a child to sometimes use the toilet—namely when it is convenient for the parents and child. Partial training really means that parents encourage their child to wear diapers some time and training pants, pull-ups, or even underwear at other times. For example, the child may be in pull-ups all morning, but in diapers during nap times. Another variation of partial training is to allow the child to choose whether to wear a diaper or underwear each morning. This means that some days the child will be wearing diapers, and other days he or she will be wearing underpants.

Separating bladder and bowel control. Parents who use this approach tackle toilet training as two distinct stages, by separating bladder control from bowel control. Although this approach may sound shocking, it is amazingly common. These parents teach their children to use the toilet for urination, but continue to use their diapers for defecation. We have several friends who considered their children "toilet trained" in that they wore underpants and urinated in the toilet, but would request a diaper each time they needed to poop.

WHY SHORT-TERM APPROACHES TO TOILET TRAINING HAVE LONG-TERM CONSEQUENCES

Although both short-term approaches to toilet training may seem like useful strategies—after all, they seem to be steps moving a child towards complete toilet training—they both represent quick-fix solutions that have long-term consequences for children and parents, and ironically, both can actually delay the accomplishment of full training. Here's why:

Creates more frequent accidents. If a child is not physically and/or emotionally ready to work on bladder and bowel control, partial training approaches are bound to fail. In turn, frequent accidents impose their own considerable costs. Accidents, and even the mere threat of accidents, cause considerable inconvenience for parents—having to travel with extra clothes (and shoes), doing additional loads of laundry, and worrying about visiting at friends' homes and public places. Quite simply, if your child is not ready for toilet training, extensive rewards and strong threats aren't going to help avoid accidents.

Children who are alternating between diapers and underpants in the partial training approach can also become confused—they may simply not remember, particularly when in the midst of needing desperately to pee, if they are wearing a diaper or underpants. Mastering bladder and bowel control involves learning to pay attention to one's internal physiological signals, which is difficult enough for a child, particularly when engaged in compelling activities (e.g., playing with friends, sleeping). Asking a child to not only pay attention to such signals but also to then assess whether they at that moment are wearing a diaper or underwear, and hence whether they need to use the toilet, is simply asking too much. I wonder how many adults could get all those demands straight one hundred percent of the time.

Children who wear absorbent pull-ups do not even experience the direct negative result of failing to use the toilet—namely feeling wet and uncomfortable—thereby making toilet training ultimately more difficult. Learning to control your bodily functions involves experiencing what happens when you have an accident—learning how it feels to pee in your pants or wake up in a wet bed—and hence children must experience how failing to use the toilet *feels* in order to learn to pay attention to their body signals and to develop such control on their own.

Leads to embarrassment. Having an accident is embarrassing for kids, and can damage their self-confidence. Children in group daycare settings are likely to feel embarrassed when they have an accident in front of their peers and need to go to the bathroom to have their clothes changed by a teacher. At home children may feel embarrassed in front of their playmates, siblings, and caregivers, especially if their friends and siblings are fully trained. This embarrassment leads some children to be reluctant to try toilet training, and to insist on using diapers full-time to avoid such problems. Similarly, children who wear underpants, but can only defecate in a diaper may feel embarrassed to have to ask for a diaper.

Delays the mastery of toilet training. It's a proven fact that the age at which toilet training begins is positively associated with only one variable—a longer *duration* of toilet training! And longer training is frustrating for kids and parents. Children's physical and emotional readiness to accomplish toilet training differs widely, but research does suggest that there is no benefit in beginning toilet training with children before twenty-seven months of age. One recent study found that children who began toilet training younger than twenty-seven months took a year or more to fully accomplish training, whereas those who started training at a later age took between five and nine months to finish. Children who habitually wet the bed at age four are also more likely to have started toilet training earlier. This is because children can't successfully accomplish bladder and bowel control until their bodies have reached a certain level of maturity.

Separating bladder from bowel control also delays mastery of toilet training, primarily because this approach sets up toilet training as a two-stage process. The fact is that most children can master bladder and bowel control at the same time, and what's more, bowel control tends to be *easier* to master (probably because bowel movements happen less frequently than does urination and are more easily held compared to urine). Children who decide to only defecate in diapers are therefore making a conscious choice based not on physical readiness but rather on emotional comfort. This explains why children who choose to defecate in diapers are fully able to ask for a diaper and to wait for the diaper to be put on prior to pooping. However, the longer a parent allows a child to make this distinction between where urination and defecation occurs, the more firmly entrenched a child becomes in defecating only in a diaper. This separation is a particularly difficult habit to break later on, delaying the completion of toilet training—and often setting up a challenging parent-child struggle.

WHY GIVING YOUR CHILD CONTROL HAS LONG-TERM ADVANTAGES

The long-term approach to toilet training focuses on giving your child control over the decision to begin using the toilet by relinquishing parental control. The long-term advantages of giving your child control are:

Enhances mastery and independence. Children who are given responsibility for choosing when to begin using the toilet gain a sense of pride, mastery, and accomplishment, and are aware that they achieved this task due to their own merits. Toilet training may in fact be the first opportunity a young child has to set a specific goal and to work towards it, and thereby experiencing the great feeling of satisfaction we all get from accomplishing a valued goal. The ability to set and work towards goals is one of the fundamental tasks of early childhood, so you need to take advantage of the natural opportunity toilet training provides.

In contrast, children who master toilet training as a result of constant pressure from their parents and not due to their own efforts are deprived of the chance to "take ownership" of this new and important skill. Similarly, children who are toilet trained through an elaborate system rewarding the accomplishment of bladder and bowel control will perceive this task as pleasing their parents' desires, not their own. So you see, children who are permitted to control their own toilet training process have the opportunity to develop the all-important sense of mastery and accomplishment.

Avoids embarrassing and inconvenient accidents. Children who are allowed to toilet train at their own pace avoid embarrassing accidents. As we saw earlier in this chapter, toilet training before a child is ready is associated with more frequent toilet training accidents, because children lack the physical and/or emotional maturity needed to manage bladder and bowel control. And these accidents are often embarrassing for children, especially when they occur in public situations. Children who are pushed to train too early thereby typically experience repeated failures, and this makes a child feel guilty, inadequate, and embarrassed. Frequent accidents can also make children understandably reluctant to wear underpants, and therefore to try to avoid toilet training altogether.

Simplifies your own life. Because an older child has the physical capacity to control their bladder and bowels, toilet training goes much faster. My older son didn't even start toilet training in earnest until he was forty months old (which at the time caused *me* much concern and embarrassment), but once we began, the entire process was accomplished in less than a week. He woke up one

Saturday morning and peed in the toilet and then decided he was ready to wear underpants. So, a delay in starting toilet training means fewer accidents for you to clean up— and trust me, it is no fun having to clean up after frequent accidents and doing endless loads of laundry. It also gets very tiring having to bring spare clothes (don't forget socks and shoes) each time you leave the house, drop your child off at school or daycare, or take a trip.

Simplifies the entire process. Children who are toilet trained at a later stage make a complete transition to bladder and bowel control, so toilet training is accomplished in only one, as opposed to two or three, steps. Some children who are trained at too early an age only learn bladder control and continue to use diapers for bowel movements, while others manage bladder and bowel control during the day but have accidents at night (necessitating diapers at night and during nap times). Once my older son switched to underwear that Saturday morning, he wore only underwear from that point on— including all night—and experienced only a few accidents over the next few weeks. Similarly, after my younger son made the switch to underpants, he wet his bed a few times in the next few months, but quickly was able to wake himself up at night to go to the toilet (or rather, to wake us up to take him to the toilet!). In contrast, many of my friends described their children as toilet trained months earlier, but their children continued to wear diapers some of the time for the reasons described above, making the toilet training process much longer.

Eliminates parent-child power struggles. Allowing your child to decide when to use the toilet eliminates unnecessary power struggles because you understand what your child already knows—that it is ultimately the child's responsibility to make this decision. Your biggest problem is to trust me (and your child) to show you that this is the reality of this developmental milestone.

THE SLOW AND STEADY APPROACH TO TOILET TRAINING

As you now know, the long-term approach to toilet training gives your child a sense of control and mastery, enhances self-esteem and independence, and at the same time, reduces your hassles and headaches. Below are the specific steps for approaching this important toddler challenge:

1. Start when you know your child is truly ready.

Even the most dedicated parent can't toilet train a child who is not ready to be toilet trained, and that even the most intelligent child cannot be toilet trained before he or she is physically ready to do so. Here are the signs to look for:

First, your child should stay dry for several hours at a time, which shows that the child is physically able to hold their urine for a set period of time. Likewise, children who have bowel movements at fairly regular times (e.g., right after lunch or before bedtime) are also ready to master toilet training.

Second, your child should prefer being dry, ideally coupled with a dislike of dirty or soggy diapers. Children who exhibit this dislike are motivated to avoid diapers completely.

Third, your child should be familiar with basic body parts and functions, such as the names your family uses to describe urination and defecation, as well as some ability to do some simple tasks related to using the toilet, such as pulling up and down their own pants.

2. Let your child take responsibility for toilet training.

Remember, early toilet training is not a sign of a child's innate intelligence or ability to master physical tasks, nor is it a sign of great parenting. All children will eventually become toilet trained so it doesn't really matter if your child does so at age two or three, or even four. Give your child every opportunity to use the toilet along with reminders to use the toilet, but leave the final decision up to him or her. When my sons complained about having to have their diaper changed, I'd point out to them that anytime they wanted to avoid diaper changes, they could simply choose to use the toilet instead. In this way, I reminded them of the option to use the toilet, but left the decision to do so entirely up to them.

3. Provide only small rewards for successful toilet use.

Don't set up elaborate rewards for using the toilet. Giving stickers or candy each time the toilet is used successfully or a larger reward for making the full transition to toilet training (such as a special new toy or a trip to a favorite restaurant), only sets up toilet training as something a child does in order to get a reward and not for its mastery. The use of such incentives can backfire because as you now know, the motivation to be toilet trained should not come from you but from your child.

4. Back off toilet training during times of stress and change.

If your family life is currently in transition (e.g., you are moving to a new house, your child is starting a new school, you are expecting a new baby), just hold off on toilet training until your child has adjusted to the transition. This is common sense. If there is even slight turmoil in the family, it's unfair to expect that your child can accomplish something as important as toilet training. After all, we adults don't do well during times of stress and change, so respect this same inability in your child. My older son Andrew was showing great interest in the toilet when he was about two-and-a-half, and had several successes in the toilet. I was thrilled, in part because I was eight months pregnant with his brother. "How wonderful," I remember saying to my mother, "that he'll be out of diapers before his sibling arrives." Wishful thinking. When Robert arrived, Andrew's interest in the toilet promptly disappeared for several months. And that was fine—we just dropped the entire topic of toilet training for several months.

5. Avoid pull-ups and highly absorbent training pants.

Pull-ups and other highly absorbent pants make it impossible for a child to experience the consequences of having an accident, which makes it more difficult for them to make the connection between the physical action of losing control of the bladder and the unpleasant consequence of feeling uncomfortable in wet pants.

6. Make toilet training an "all or nothing" event.

Decide if your child is going to wear underpants or diapers and stick with that decision. Otherwise you are setting your child up for failure because it is hard for them to remember what they are wearing. For example, a child who learns that urine goes in the toilet but continues to make bowel movements in diapers must in reality be trained twice. Similarly, a child who wears underwear during the day but diapers at night and during nap times may have trouble distinguishing between when they need to use the toilet and when they don't. It is better for them to wear underwear and have some accidents (which will remind them to use the toilet), than to confuse them by switching to diapers at different times. This switching may make sense to you, but it won't to your child.

Remember, too, that children who are wearing underpants should be urinating as well as defecating in a toilet. By allowing your child to poop in a diaper you are fostering fears about defecating in the toilet, which will only get more entrenched over time. If a child is not ready to poop in a toilet yet, stick with diapers.

7. Make a quick transition from potty seat to regular toilet.

Some children become fixated on only using the particular potty in their own home, and are unwilling or unable to use a regular toilet in other settings. This effectively means that even a fully trained child will have accidents in other settings in which their special potty is not available—at a mall, in a restaurant, or at Grandma's house.

Perhaps a few weeks or a month after your child has been fully-trained, make a focused effort to eliminate using the potty and encourage using the regular toilet. This may not be easy. Kids are very persistent when they put their minds to something. So be prepared to resort to drastic measures, if needed! In my case, my older son was willing to pee in the toilet, but not to defecate. After buying him a special stool to rest his feet so he felt secure while he sat on the regular toilet, we decided "enough was enough." I hid the potty in the basement and told him the potty was broken and the plumber had taken it away. He proceeded not to poop at all for two days (which caused my husband considerable concern), but on day three he finally pooped in the toilet. He never asked for his potty again.

8. Avoid schools that require toilet training.

Some preschools and daycare centers require that children be out of diapers before they can attend and that may push for premature toilet training. When my older son had just turned three, I signed him up for a two-week summer camp that met each morning from 8:30 to 12:30 and required all campers to be fully trained. Because he was not using the toilet with any sort of regularity, I put him in highly absorbent training pants, kept my fingers crossed that he would only pee during the morning, and explained to the counselors that he was sometimes nervous about using the toilet in public situations. We both got through the two-week camp with our secret safe, but obviously this short-term "solution" won't work if you work and need to enroll your child in permanent daycare.

9. Relax.

Have you ever met an adult who wasn't toilet trained? So relax, your child will not be the first to go to college, or high school, or even kindergarten, wearing diapers. Although it may seem like you're changing diapers forever, remember that toilet training is a major physical and psychological challenge, and kids only accomplish this task when they are able to do it. Sit back, relax, and wait for your child to take the lead—it may be longer in coming than you expected, but it will happen. It won't take longer than if you tried to begin training earlier, and it will go easier and be a positive, confidence-building experience.

Chapter 8
Dealing With Discipline

Disciplining your child is one of the toughest tasks in parenting. This is, in part, because effective discipline requires considerable time and energy from us already overworked parents. Although managing discipline is a formidable challenge, it presents us with yet another opportunity to help increase our children's independence and self-reliance and foster the bond we have with our children. The slow and steady approach to discipline may, at least initially, be challenging for you, but I promise that the benefits will be well worth it.

THE CHALLENGE OF DISCIPLINE

One reason that discipline is so difficult is because we desperately want our children to engage in positive behavior, so we are often tempted to rely on quick-fix solutions that lead to pleasant outcomes. Think about it—how many times have you fallen unintentionally into this trap of giving in to your child's desires to avoid conflict by extending bedtimes, buying the candy your child wants at the checkout line, or giving into pleas to watch television or videos? In every one of these cases, and others too numerous to mention, the quick-fix solution of giving in to your child's demands is done because it's the easier choice at that moment.

The pressure to rely on these quick-fixes is especially strong when you're in public settings and enforcing limits may prove awkward and embarrassing. A classic example we have all experienced is the horror of a temper tantrum in public. Here's the familiar scenario: You are in the checkout line paying for groceries, and your child is begging for some desirable toy or treat and his emotions escalate. You really want your child to stop screaming, kicking, and rolling on the floor—you don't want to look like an idiot in front of the other shoppers. What do you do? At that precise moment—with strangers looking on—we choose the quick-fix. "OK, I'll buy the toy, if you stop crying." I can't disagree that buying a screaming child a toy in a store feels like a small price to pay for avoiding the child's tears and your own embarrassment at having your parenting skills evaluated in public. But have no doubt about it, kids can sense when you are most vulnerable to caving in to their demands in a public situation, and they know how to exploit this to their advantage. But it works for parents, too, in the short-term.

WHY SHORT-TERM DISCIPLINE HAS LONG-TERM CONSEQUENCES

Relying on quick-fix approaches to discipline leads to substantial long-term consequences, including:

Creating negative behavior patterns. Children form associations very quickly, so remember that once a child is rewarded for unacceptable behavior, you've almost guaranteed that he or she will continue this type of negative behavior later on—after all, it came with a reward! Bear in mind that the reward needn't be tangible in terms of a toy or candy. Just paying lots of attention to your child for making the demand—and throwing the tantrum—also reinforces this behavior. When one of my friend's daughters would misbehave, she would count backwards from one hundred to one before enforcing the consequence, usually a time out. This also meant that all conversation between adults and all activity would stop while she counted very slowly: one hundred, ninety-nine, ninety-eight, ninety-seven . . . What my friend didn't realize was that her solution had the exact opposite outcome from what she intended. What she actually did was reinforce this misbehavior by making her daughter the center of attention of everyone in the room, single-handedly putting an end to all other activity!

Inconsistent discipline, or discipline accompanied by empty threats, also creates bad behavior. This method involves threatening your child with a particular consequence for engaging in a behavior, but then failing to follow through on your threat. You've probably seen a parent use this type of an approach—or maybe you do it yourself. It goes like this: A parent in a restaurant tells their child that if he or she screams again, they will have to leave the restaurant. The child screams again, and the threat is made again, and the cycle continues over and over again. If you set a rule but can't follow through on the consequences when it is violated, your child quickly learns not to take your words seriously. The threat then loses its power. In fact, the hardest type of behavior to stop is behavior that is inconsistently reinforced—because sometimes doing the behavior will actually get the child a reward, he or she will keep repeating the behavior in hopes that it will finally pay off. Inconsistent reinforcement is the type of reinforcement that slot machines provide, and, as any gambler will tell you, it is almost impossible to stop putting quarters in a machine because you just keep hoping you'll win the jackpot.

Impairing the parent-child attachment bond. This is a tricky one—it defies logic that giving in to all of your child's needs leads to attachment problems. What happens is that under the guise of being considerate to a child's immediate needs, you can become overly permissive which actually shows a lack of sensitivity and responsiveness. Are you with me? Here's why: Young children, unable to manage their behavior entirely on their own, desperately need their parents to set limits so they learn to act in an appropriate manner. For example, sleepy and cranky children never seem to recognize that they need to sleep. They need *us* to recognize this need and teach them what to do when they are tired. When we fail to set and enforce these limits, we are ignoring our kids' fundamental needs and our role as teacher. This lack of attention to setting boundaries leads kids to doubt our love for them, and undermines the parent-child attachment bond.

WHY IGNORING BAD BEHAVIOR HAS LONG-TERM CONSEQUENCES

If you think ignoring bad behavior is a good discipline strategy precisely because it fails to reward behavior designed primarily to gain attention, think again. Simply ignoring bad behavior is not good discipline because it:

Fails to teach children appropriate behavior. If your child is engaging in a behavior that is unacceptable simply because they want to—such as kicking the back of your seat in the car or making an irritating noise—and you choose to ignore this bad behavior, you are failing to constructively teach your child appropriate manners and behavior. Ignoring this bad behavior ensures that your child isn't learning that this behavior is unacceptable, and he or she will therefore continue to engage in this type of activity in the future.

Ignoring bad behavior can even lead to an escalation of the behavior because children who lack clear rules may try to figure out what the adults' expectations are for their behavior, and may then act out in an effort to find some limits themselves. In other words, children may deliberately (perhaps unconsciously) misbehave in an attempt to force us to eventually show a reaction. A study done with preschool children found that the teachers who failed to set clear and consistent rules encountered much more misbehavior from children later on than the teachers who had clearly stated and consistently enforced rules for acceptable behavior. Interestingly, the connection between inconsistent rule-setting and enforcement with misbehavior was particularly strong for boys (which means we parents of sons must be especially diligent).

Fosters a feeling of insecurity. Ignoring our kids—even when they are behaving poorly—gives kids the impression that we don't care, leading them to feel less secure about our love and concern for them. After all, ignoring bad behavior means ignoring your child. Just remember how you feel when you are ignored by someone—perhaps a friend or even your spouse—after a major disagreement. Being ignored is not a good feeling.

WHY SETTING AND ENFORCING RULES HAS LONG-TERM ADVANTAGES

It is my belief that one of our most important responsibilities as parents is helping our kids learn to manage their own behavior—a crucial skill for succeeding at home and school—and that parents can best accomplish this goal by setting and enforcing rules in a warm and caring way. This approach leads to a number of benefits for you and your kids:

Enhances children's self-reliance and independence. Setting and enforcing clear and consistent rules assists our kids in learning how to manage their own behavior. In using this long-term approach we need to not only set and enforce specific rules, but also to take time to explain to our kids the motivation for these rules. For example, I once had to stop my child from eating too many cookies. He understood my intent when I reminded him that after Curious George, in the classic tale of *Curious George and the Chocolate Factory,* ate too many chocolates, he developed an awful stomach ache. If he continued to eat cookies he wouldn't feel good either, I told him, and I would never want him to experience such pain. You might tell your child that an 8 PM bedtime is important so that they will feel happy and refreshed when they wake up in the morning, and that sleeping provides their body with a chance to rest and grow. By providing reasons for our rules we help our children internalize appropriate standards for behavior, which will help them act appropriately in setting and knowing their own limits even when we're not around. This skill will serve them well all through life.

Fosters a strong parent-child attachment bond. Setting clear limits on your child's behavior provides a clear signal to your child that you are aware of and responsive to their needs and are concerned about their well-being. Not doing this is the same as if your boss simply told you to "do your job" but didn't make clear what was expected of you—the types of tasks that were to be your responsibility, how long various tasks should take, or even how your work would be evaluated. Imagine how uncomfortable such a system would make you feel. We all, no matter what our age, need clear expectations. By setting limits you help your kids learn appropriate standards of behavior while showing love and concern for their well-being and happiness.

THE SLOW AND STEADY APPROACH TO DISCIPLINE

The goal of parental discipline is to create children who have a strong sense of attachment to their parents and a strong sense of independence and self-reliance. Here's how you can do this:

1. Acknowledge your child's views.

Kids throw tantrums when they think their needs are misunderstood or ignored. Put yourself in a child's shoes: They simply don't understand why they must leave the playground at that precise moment, why you won't buy them that candy bar, and why they have to brush their teeth. In turn, they can—and often do—experience all of these events as frustrating, which in turn can lead to a tantrum. This is much the same feeling as we experience when our spouse refuses a request from us for some help and doesn't even offer an explanation.

Simply acknowledging that you hear what your child is asking and that you will try your best to fulfill those needs in some way, goes a long way towards reducing temper tantrums. Follow these simple rules: Tell your children exactly why they can't have what they want at that moment in language they can understand, then try to offer a substitute choice so they feel their needs are valued. For example, you might refuse to buy a toy because you don't have enough money with you, but make it clear that the toy will be added to a "wish list" for purchase for a birthday or holiday. This act tells your child that you understand and empathize with his or her desires, and lets them feel independent and in control of their choices.

2. Allow your child to make choices.

Children have relatively low levels of control over their environment since they cannot choose the place they live, where they go to school, what they eat, and so on. But children need to have opportunities to make decisions on their own and to follow through on these decisions. In turn, one of the crucial ways that you can foster your child's independence is by allowing him or her to exercise control over daily life decisions. Whenever possible, give your child choices, such as which cup to drink from, which book to read, or what type of cereal to eat.

Allowing your child to make some decisions independently can go a long way towards eliminating temper tantrums. I remember my husband coming downstairs very frustrated with our then two-year-old Robert, who was refusing to change out of his pajamas into the shirt my husband had selected for him to wear. I asked Bart to bring me any two shirts from Robert's dresser, and promptly asked Robert which shirt he'd prefer wearing. Robert eagerly pointed to one of the shirts (ironically enough, it was the one my husband had originally selected), and was quickly dressed. In sum, don't underestimate the power of offering a choice.

3. Pick your battles.

Some parent-child battles are unavoidable since we parents must set rules about safety (wearing seatbelts), physical health (brushing teeth before bed), and daily schedules (attending preschool or daycare). These are all examples of how we exercise control over our child's choice, which is exactly what sets up a power struggle. Although some conflicts are unavoidable, others are not—so we all need to think carefully about the specific rules we set. For example, you may rightly refuse your child's request to wear a sundress and sandals in the middle of a snowstorm, but if your child insists on wearing the same worn and ratty shoes every day instead of his brand-new sneakers, try to let him. My younger son wore a Patriots football uniform—pants and jersey—virtually every day for three months when he was three, which was endlessly embarrassing for me, but a source of great pride and satisfaction for him. In sum, honor the decisions you can.

4. Only set rules you are willing to enforce.

Children who learn that breaking a rule has specific and undesirable consequences are much less likely to violate this rule—as well as other rules—in the future. I remember inviting another family to come out to dinner with us when my son Andrew was two-and-a-half. Their sons were playing in the sandbox at our house with Andrew, who was starting to toss sand. My husband warned him that sand needs to stay near the ground, but shortly after, he threw a huge ball of sand on one of his friends, who promptly started to cry. We apologized to our friends, took Andrew to his room, and did not go to the restaurant that evening. Was it awkward? Yes. Was it embarrassing? Yes. Did Andrew learn that we really meant what we said? Yes. And that is the reason it was all worth it. In sum, don't make a threat if you don't realistically think you can follow through on it.

5. Be consistent.

Discipline your kids in a consistent way—whether at home or in public, with friends or with your in-laws—

because inconsistently reinforced behavior sends mixed messages and results in behavior that is extremely hard to change. Consistent discipline is very hard—precisely because it involves consistent behavior from us parents. Never forget that the costs of inconsistent discipline, including continued bad (and even escalating) behavior and a disruption in the parent-child attachment bond, carry too high a price for you and your kids.

Chapter 9
Learning Life Skills

One of the constant challenges parents face, particularly in the preschool years, is how to teach our kids important new life skills, such as drinking out of a cup without a lid, getting dressed, and cleaning up after themselves. Teaching life skills is a crucial part of helping kids gain independence because these skills show kids they can do things on their own, without needing to depend on us or on other adults. Although helping kids develop these skills can be a long and even frustrating process, by taking a long-term approach you will increase your child's self-esteem, strengthen the attachment bond, and simplify your life.

THE CHALLENGE OF
TEACHING LIFE SKILLS

Think about how many times in the last week you did something for your children that they could learn to do on their own—cleaning their room, getting dressed, pouring milk, and so on. But doing these tasks ourselves is easier and faster than taking the time to teach our kids (or, once learned, to do it themselves). The temptation to rely on short-term choices is especially strong when you are trying to help your child master complex new skills, like riding a bike or swimming, because frankly teaching these complex skills is really hard work. One of the toughest (physical and mental) challenges I faced with my five-year-old was teaching him to ride a bicycle without training wheels. My husband took off the training wheels, and Andrew and I set out down the street, him pedaling slowly and me running slowly after him, hunched over and holding on desperately to the back of the bicycle. My back hurt, my feet hurt, and anytime Andrew tipped over slightly, he became concerned that he was going to fall and stopped pedaling completely. In watching all of this action, my husband announced that I was crazy, and that we should get those training wheels back on promptly and give up on riding without training wheels for another year (or longer). And at that moment, the training wheels approach definitely seemed much easier for me, and for Andrew! This is a classic example of how parents are often tempted to use short-cuts in teaching skills.

WHY PUTTING OFF TEACHING SKILLS HAS LONG-TERM CONSEQUENCES

Despite the appeal of taking a short-term approach, remember that simply delaying the real work involved in teaching life skills can have long-term consequences. Here's what's wrong with delaying teaching important life skills:

Interferes with the development of self-reliance. If you continue to help your child with skills that he should be doing on his own, you are depriving him of the opportunity to practice—and thereby perfect—these new skills. A child who doesn't learn how to manage a real cup without spilling, or does not know how to put on their own clothes, is not becoming self-reliant. Although we may think we are doing our children a favor by simply performing a task for them, we are actually making them dependent on us, and thereby interfering with the very important task of developing self-reliance. There will be a price to pay for this lack of self-reliance when your child enters school settings and is expected to be fairly independent.

Interferes with the development of the new skill. In some cases a reliance on a quick-fix solution to teaching our kids a complex skill can even impair their ability to successfully learn this skill later on—because the quick-fix solution actually teaches them something they must later unlearn. For example, kids who learn to drink out of a sippy cup that is designed to be "unspillable" will have trouble later on understanding how to keep other sippy cups from spilling. Similarly, my brother taught swimming lessons for many years, and reported that the hardest child to teach to swim independently is a child who has first "learned" how to swim with "floaties" around their arms. By keeping the children's arms above water, these devices allow children to bounce around in relatively deep water without fear. But the problem with using these devices is that they do not allow a child to learn strategies for water safety by using their arms and legs to stay afloat. And when children are taught that they can go in the pool only when they have these devices on their arms—which only cements this dependency—it makes the already tough job of teaching a child to swim independently without floaties even harder. In both cases, the short-term quick-fix approach must be unlearned before the real skill is mastered.

Interferes with the development of peer relationships. It can be awkward or embarrassing for children when their peers have mastered skills that they have not. Imagine your child needing help putting on her jacket when the other kids in her preschool can do this by themselves, or spilling milk because he doesn't know how to pour from a pitcher at snack time when his peers don't have any trouble with this task. Preschool children very quickly notice differences in what they and their peers can do, and feel embarrassed when their own skills are clearly lagging behind those of other kids.

Creates a parent-child power struggle. Children who haven't learned how to perform a given skill are completely dependent on their parents for assistance. A child who needs help getting dressed in the morning, or tying their shoes, for example, probably needs you to perform these skills when you are also trying to simultaneously make breakfast, fix school lunches, and perhaps drink a cup of coffee. It's unfair to get angry or lose patience with a child (yet that's what we tend to do) if they need us to do something that we have not taken the time to teach them to do on their own.

WHY TAKING TIME TO TEACH SKILLS HAS LONG-TERM ADVANTAGES

Teaching your child how to master new skills has many long-term benefits. Here's what is good about teaching your child to be age-appropriately self-sufficient:

Enhances children's self-esteem. When you take the time to teach your child new skills, you are helping them master new tasks and in turn experience feelings of great pride. Remember that children get tremendous satisfaction from mastering new skills—even very mundane skills like zipping their coats, cleaning their own rooms, and pooping in the toilet! One of our friends' daughters, Alexandra, learned how to tie her shoes when she was only four-years-old. She would then proudly display this skill at any opportunity, eager to show amazed adults that she could do it. Similarly, although Andrew struggled mightily with learning how to ride a bicycle without training wheels, he was thrilled when he eventually mastered this task.

Enhances the parent-child attachment bond. Working on a task with your child is a great way of spending quality time together as well as demonstrating to your child that you are available for support whenever needed—thereby strengthening the attachment bond. For example, if you are helping your child learn how to dress herself, you can let her struggle with figuring out which arm goes in which hole while you provide helpful verbal guidance and encouragement. This approach allows your children the freedom to practice important lifetime skills on their own, but also shows that you are responsive to their needs.

Simplifies your life. Because children who have mastered age-appropriate skills are much more self-reliant, teaching skills to them means they won't need to rely on you for assistance. Just imagine how much easier your life could be if you didn't have to dress your child, brush their teeth, clean their rooms, etc.

THE SLOW AND STEADY APPROACH TO TEACHING NEW SKILLS

The slow and steady approach to teaching your child new skills is easily done by:

1. Teaching in small, easy-to-follow steps.

Set small, achievable goals so your child will experience success and pride, and minimize frustration and disappointment. Do this by breaking large skills into smaller ones, and only focusing on a single small step at a time. For example, first teach your child to brush her teeth by showing her how to squeeze toothpaste onto her brush, next rubbing the brush across each of her teeth, and finally practice rinsing her mouth. Show these steps by demonstrating them yourself. Kids are great mimics—use this behavior to your advantage. However, make sure your child is able to master each of the steps before you attempt to teach a particular skill—if they can't do all the steps required to complete the skill, they will only be frustrated and that is not the goal.

2. Providing opportunities for practicing new skills.

Providing kids with the opportunity to practice new skills is an important step because with all skills, one gets better with practice. Think back to when you learned how to drive a car—can you remember when it was very difficult to remember all the different steps: which pedal to push with which foot, how to use your mirrors to drive in reverse, when to brake, etc. The first few times you drove, with nervous passengers no doubt, you probably weren't so smooth at putting all the steps together. But now, after years of practice, driving takes little, if any, effort. It's the same thing for kids as they learn to master each and every new skill, from tying their shoes to buttoning their shirts to using a fork. Give them frequent opportunities to practice so that these skills become automatic and effortless.

3. Creating opportunities for success.

Help your child maintain confidence by creating opportunities to successfully experience the mastering of a new skill. If you are trying to teach your child to dress herself, buy clothes that are easy for a child to get on and off. This means buying clothes with few buttons, shoes with Velcro straps instead of laces, and clothes in a larger size to make them easier to get into and out of. Similarly, if you are trying to teach your child how to ride a bicycle, buy a very small bicycle so that your child can learn balancing skills while being able to easily touch two feet to the ground when needed. Once the skill is learned on the little bicycle, it can then be easily transferred to a larger bicycle.

4. Rewarding the effort, not the results.

It's important to remember that children's early efforts when trying virtually any skill will fall somewhat short of perfection, and that it is very important not to discourage these early attempts. Maintain enthusiasm while practicing new skills by praising every effort, not just the outcome. This means you should be willing to tolerate spills, be happy with a somewhat clean room, and expect loosely-tied laces. Perfection is not your goal.

5. Keeping your eye on the long-term goal.

Teaching a new skill is rarely, if ever, easy. The trick is to support a child who will probably get discouraged. Don't let this discouragement frustrate you and don't, even though it may be tempting, choose a quick-fix to make life easier. At these moments, remember to focus on the goal you are ultimately trying to achieve, and choose an approach that will lead to the best long-term outcome. Cleaning your child's room by yourself teaches him that you will take care of his mess. This may be easier in the short-term, but not in the long-term because you've taken responsibility for something that your child should be learning to do on her own.

Part 4

SPECIAL ISSUES
ACROSS THE YEARS

Chapter 10
The Childcare Dilemma

Let's face it—we parents struggle to figure out how best to combine raising our kids with some type of paid work outside the home. Although I can't make balancing work and family easy, I can promise that making a long-term choice about managing this balance will lead to lasting advantages for you and your kids. A long-term choice doesn't mean avoiding all paid childcare, nor does it mean quitting your job: It just means thinking through the real costs and benefits of various childcare

127

options, and making an informed choice that works best for you and your child.

THE CHALLENGE OF CHILDCARE

Stopping all paid work while our kids are young is simply not an option for most of us—not if we want to make the mortgage payments, put food on the table, and take a vacation every now and then. Even in families that can afford a one parent income, both parents may want to pursue some type of work outside the home—to maintain professional connections, to experience a sense of fulfillment, and/or to provide disposable income for the family.

For working parents, finding good and reliable childcare is always a challenge. It's comforting to know you're not alone in this quest, and that quality childcare is available (although not necessarily easy to find). 54 percent of families with employed mothers use center-based or family daycare for their three to four-year-olds, and 33 percent rely on such care for children younger than age three. Although childcare most typically includes a daycare center or a family daycare setting, approximately 4 percent of children are cared for in their own homes by a nanny or babysitter. But, as in all parenting situations, you need to be aware of the benefits as well as costs of different childcare options, which will help you select the childcare situation that works best for your family.

WHY USING SHORT-TERM APPROACHES TO CHILDCARE CAN BE VERY APPEALING

Full-time childcare, either through a daycare or an in-home childcare provider, enables both parents to return to work full-time shortly after the baby's birth. Some families may need the income of both parents, but even in those families that could get by on only one paycheck, the parents may fear that taking an extended leave, or returning to work on a part-time basis, will impair their career advancement. Full-time childcare also allows parents to avoid the potential resentment that could arise if one parent (typically the husband) returns to full-time work while the other parent (typically the wife) remains at home with the child.

Moreover, many people, not surprisingly, find giving full-time care to their children exhausting, and hence choose some type of paid childcare. When my sons were infants and I stayed home with them full-time, I remember feeling envious of my husband as he set off for his job. For stay-at-home parents, many mundane aspects of office life—such as having a relaxing cup of coffee, going to the bathroom alone, and surfing the Internet over lunch—can all seem like fantasies. Parents may also believe that full-time childcare during the week allows them the opportunity to provide a higher quality of care during the times they are interacting with their child in the evenings and on weekends.

Parents may also believe that aspects of paid childcare could be beneficial to their child. If you have relatively little experience taking care of infants and small children, you might even see full-time care provided by an in-home nanny or daycare worker as in some ways superior to the care you could provide on your own. A paid childcare worker is, after all, likely to have some specialized training and extensive experience in working with children.

But despite the appeal of paid childcare situations, both daycare settings and in-home caregiver situations can have unforeseen consequences for both kids and parents.

WHY DAYCARE CAN HAVE LONG-TERM CONSEQUENCES

Many parents think that daycare provides important opportunities for their kids to socialize with other children, and to thereby gain skills in cooperation and sharing. Although the perceived advantages of daycare settings lead many parents to rely on this type of childcare, a growing amount of evidence suggests that many daycare settings are simply not the best choice, especially for infants and very young children. Daycare settings can:

Create behavioral problems. Children who spend time in daycare settings show higher levels of behavioral problems, including aggression with peers and parents. One recent study by the National Institute of Health and Human Development examined more than one thousand children ages one to three-and-a-half. The findings from this study revealed that the more hours a child spent in daycare, the higher the incidence of problem behavior later on, and the greater severity of such problems. In fact, the amount of time spent in daycare was a stronger predictor of behavior problems than the quality of the care received. Children who spend more time in daycare also engage in lower levels of positive social behavior with other children than those who spend little to no time. Ironically, even children who spend large amounts of time with other children do not appear to benefit in terms of learning skills related to sharing and cooperation.

Interestingly, daycare has a particularly negative effect on children who have a strong bond with their parents. One study found that children who have a secure attachment to their caregiver at age one and are then placed in a daycare setting show higher rates of negative and avoidant behavior at age three-and-a-half. They are also rated as more aggressive by the kindergarten teachers. In contrast, children who are insecurely attached at age one, seem to benefit from daycare, and actually become more independent and less withdrawn. Although this finding may seem surprising, it makes sense if you consider the different experiences daycare settings are likely to have on secure versus insecurely attached children. For secure children, who have a strong bond with their parents, placement in a daycare setting may make them feel angry and abandoned by their parents. They would likely prefer to be spending time with their parents instead of in a daycare situation. In contrast, children who have not developed a secure attachment bond with their parents may finally be able to develop such a bond with their caregivers in a daycare setting.

Creates high levels of stress. One reason why children in daycare settings show higher levels of behavioral problems is that this type of childcare can create high levels of stress, especially in very young children. In line with this view, there is physiological proof that young children experience stress in daycare situations: A study conducted by researchers at the University of Minnesota revealed that in children younger than age three, levels of the hormone cortisol, which is a sign of stress, increase in the afternoon as children spend more time in daycare settings. In contrast, levels of cortisol decrease in the afternoon when these children are at home. So, children may benefit from some exposure to group daycare settings, but may experience high levels of stress when they must spend extended time in this setting. Levels of cortisol are particularly high in children who are shy, meaning these children may be particularly at risk of developing stress-related problems from spending time in daycare.

And it makes sense that daycare settings—which obviously involve large numbers of children and several different caregivers—could be especially stressful for children who are less comfortable with social interactions. Children who are in full-time daycare, meaning 9 AM to 5 PM five days a week, are actually spending more time in a group setting than children in elementary school, who typically attend only from 8:30 AM to 3:30 PM five days a week. Can it possibly be beneficial for small children to spend forty hours a week in a group daycare setting?

Daycare settings can also lead to stress because children must get used to not only interacting with many other kids, but also interacting with different teachers. Moreover, as you've probably heard, childcare workers have extremely high turn over rates—many daycare workers make job changes every year or even more frequently. During my younger son's first year in a daycare setting, four different teachers quit working in his classroom during a twelve-month period! This means that all of the children constantly faced adjusting to new teachers, with distinct styles, routines, and personalities, every few months. And this is sadly not an unusual occurrence in daycare settings.

Creates health problems. Daycare settings are also associated with a number of health problems, including infectious diseases as well as injuries. In fact, one study in the *Journal of the American Medical Association* found that preschool-aged children who are in daycare settings are two to four times as likely to experience an infectious disease as those who are cared for at home. Children who are cared for in their own homes are simply much less likely to be exposed to the numerous bugs that travel around daycare settings.

WHY IN-HOME CHILDCARE CAN HAVE LONG-TERM CONSEQUENCES

The choice to hire either a live-in or live-out nanny instead of relying on a daycare center can provide some important advantages over daycare settings, particularly if you have unpredictable work schedules or put in long hours on the job. Nannies are likely to have greater flexibility in their hours, can also provide care to a sick child, and ensure that your child will receive more individualized care than would occur in a group daycare setting. Although hiring a full-time caregiver to come to your own home avoids some of the problems associated with daycare settings, this approach has its own potential for long-term consequences.

In-home caregivers have their own distinct ideas about child rearing. This difference makes it impossible to provide exactly the same type of care you would provide.

By hiring a nanny, you are allowing someone to make their own judgments about the way they will care for and discipline your child. Hiring a paid caregiver is not just hiring someone to raise your child exactly as you would choose to do so yourself—it is hiring someone to make their own choices about how to raise your child, for better or for worse. Think: Would you want your nanny to answer your child's questions about God or explain where babies come from? You also need to keep careful watch to make sure this is the type of nanny who takes your child to the library and not just to the mall. In addition, a nanny may express negative stereotypes about other people to your child, even in a subtle way, influencing the way your child perceives the world, which may go against your beliefs.

In-home caregivers are likely to rely on short-term solutions to common childcare challenges. Since this type of caregiving may also carry the responsibility for assisting with household chores, such as cooking, laundry, and cleaning, there may not be time to give your children full-time attention. This leads to relying on many of the quick-fix solutions that ultimately lead to long-term problems, including giving children unhealthy foods, plugging in pacifiers, and using television and videos to entertain. Remember, it's the rare paid childcare worker who has the same type of love and concern about your child that you do, or who is as focused on the long-term consequences of their short-term fixes.

In-home caregivers are unlikely to provide continual care. As we already saw with daycare workers, in-home caregivers also have extremely high turn over rates—many nannies make job changes every year. A nanny who particularly likes caring for babies, for example, may find a new family to work for after your adorable infant reaches the "terrible twos." Moreover, when caregivers move to a new job, they may give only a few weeks notice, which is unlikely to be enough time for you to find a good replacement or to prepare your child for the change in caregivers.

WHY TAKING A LONG-TERM APPROACH TO CHILDCARE HAS LONG-TERM ADVANTAGES

A long-term approach to childcare is based in the belief that parents provide the most attentive, affectionate, and consistent care to their children, especially their very young children, and that translates to the following benefits:

Enhances the parent-child attachment bond. By taking primary care of your child when she is very young, you are providing her with consistent and caring attention, demonstrating to her that you are there when she needs you, and showing unconditional love and support as she experiences her very first relationship. No matter how loving a paid childcare worker may seem, she (and yes, most of them are women!) will not have the same type of warmth and attachment to your child as a parent.

Providing primary care for your child is not only good for him, but is also good for you: You get to know your child better by spending real quality time together—not just the brief time between the end of your work day and your child's bedtime. Just ask yourself how you will feel when you miss seeing their various accomplishments—the first smile, the first word, the first step.

Enhances children's intellectual development. Because parents alone are uniquely focused on providing benefits for their own children, we are much more likely to make child raising choices that enhance our children's intellectual development—to read numerous books to our kids, to encourage their persistence on a challenging puzzle, and to answer their *many* questions.

THE SLOW AND STEADY APPROACH TO MANAGING THE CHILDCARE CHALLENGE

For those of you who are thinking about using paid childcare, here are ways to avoid, or at least minimize, your reliance on paid childcare as well as to select the very highest quality.

1. Stay home for as long as possible.

Staying home with an infant and/or small child is not an easy job—this is why many parents who could take a longer leave or arrange a part-time work schedule choose not to. Even though you won't realize it now, spending time with your infant is one of the best ways of forming a secure attachment bond. It's true that the early childhood years pass very, very quickly, and many parents who miss this early time with their children later regret having not spent more time with them. Conversely, you'd be hard pressed to find the parent who stayed home with their child who regrets that decision. Given that we know the importance of spending this early time with your children, you should do what you can for one of you to stay at home with your baby—if not for years, at least for as long as you can.

2. Minimize the use of paid childcare.

Even once you need to return to work, do what you can to minimize the amount of time your baby must spend in a paid childcare setting. Many employers now allow parents to return to work on a reduced schedule, either permanently or temporarily. I have several friends who've returned to work four days a week (at 80 percent pay) instead of five. This may seem like a small difference, but over the course of a year, it adds up to fifty extra days spent with your baby. After the birth of my first child, I arranged my class schedule so that I only taught in the mornings, and could therefore spend most afternoons with him. Employers may also allow you to work from home at least part-time, which can reduce the need to introduce full-time childcare, or at least allow you to spend more time with your baby. My sister-in-law returned to work only four days a week following the birth of my niece, Jane, and was able to work one of these days from home. Thus, she was away from the baby only three days per week, not five. The next best thing is to enlist a grandparent, sibling, or other close family member, to help part-time with childcare early on. Before you decide to go back to work, know that even though the loss of income will interfere with some family goals, these short-term sacrifices are priceless in terms of their long-term benefits.

3. Choose daycare centers and in-home caregivers that meet the highest quality standards.

If you simply cannot afford to stop work completely, work part-time, or work from home, you need to invest in the highest quality childcare possible. Whether it is an in-home caregiver or a daycare setting, here is what you should look for when evaluating childcare options.

Daycare: Select a center that meets the highest quality standards—which only 10 to 15 percent of centers do. Although specific guidelines for childcare centers vary from state to state, top quality centers all share some common features. First, a small teacher-child ratio provides for as much individual attention as possible even in a group daycare setting. Ideal ratios for very young children, under eighteen months, are one adult to every three children, in a setting of no more than six children in all. For children age eighteen to twenty-six months, ratios of one to four are appropriate, with no more than twelve children in all. These ratios are above the minimum standards in virtually all states, meaning that many daycare centers will have a much higher ratio—and consequently less individual attention for your child. My children started group daycare when they were eighteen months, and I found only a single center in our town with the highest quality ratio standards—the others all simply used the lowest required by the state. The rate of teacher turn over is another important factor—you want your child to have the most consistent childcare possible, which is difficult to provide if teachers are constantly leaving for new jobs. Low turn over is also a good sign that teachers are satisfied with their work environment. Parents should also be able to visit the center at any time. Last, but certainly not least, teachers at daycare centers should have some specialized training in caring for infants and children. In top quality centers, teachers may all have college degrees in education-related fields, and perhaps even advanced degrees.

In-home caregivers: If you have chosen to hire a full-time caregiver, remember that you are choosing someone who will be with your child full-time, and that this person will play a major role in teaching and caring for your child—in fact, this person will interact with your child during more of his or her waking hours than you yourself will. Screen and interview many possible candidates before making a decision. Check all references carefully. Choose someone who shares at least some of your basic values and beliefs about child rearing, including what your child should eat, the use of television and videos, and methods of discipline. When my children were very little—younger than eighteen months—I hired college students to babysit for four or five hours each day so that I could work. These students were intelligent and articulate, extremely responsible, and truly loved working with kids. And because they were only working a few hours a day, they were less likely to become bored and turn to quick-fix approaches.

4. Introduce childcare transitions gradually.

When a decision is made, at any age, to start a child in a group daycare setting or with an in-home caregiver, you should try to introduce this change gradually.

Daycare: To make the transition to daycare go smoothly, help your child adjust in a gradual way. I recommend starting by making a few visits to daycare with your child. Begin by showing your child the available activities in the room. On the fourth or fifth visit, move away to a different part of the room to allow your child to interact with the teacher and other children in a more independent way. If your child seems comfortable in this environment, let your child know that you'll be away for thirty minutes or an hour, and return promptly after this time away. Eventually your child will be ready for you to leave him or her for a longer block of time. This type of gradual introduction to the daycare setting will make for a smooth transition to this new environment.

The staff at the daycare center may also have helpful suggestions for making the transition to daycare a smooth one. My children's daycare center asked all families to bring in photographs that could be displayed in the classroom for children to refer to as needed throughout the day. My older son was also allowed to call me at times when he was feeling sad and simply needed to hear my voice.

In-home caregiver: If you are planning on hiring an in-home caregiver, pay that person to come first for a few mornings a week so that he or she can get to know your child (and vice versa). As with the transition to a daycare center, you should ideally be present with the child and the caregiver, but then try to back away from the action to let them get acquainted. After your child seems comfortable in this situation, you could try to leave the house for short periods of time, and then only gradually leave your child for the entire day. For example, a child who has been cared for entirely at home by a parent might begin to spend two or three mornings with another caregiver for the first few weeks, and only gradually spend longer amounts of time with the new caregiver.

5. Leave your child with other caregivers on a regular basis.

Even if one of you is staying home full-time, it is also important to your child to experience other caregivers on a regular basis. Part of forming a secure attachment bond involves proving to your child that sometimes you will go away, but that you will always return. Even the most dedicated and caring at-home parent will at times need to run errands, get a hair cut, or go shopping. These regular separations, even for short periods of time, are crucial in helping your child understand that leaving him or her home with other caregivers doesn't mean you won't return.

If you are concerned about the expense of hiring sitters, many high school or college students are interested in babysitting for a little extra money, and can be hired for an hour or two once a week. If you are very nervous about leaving your child with a non-family member, keep a cell phone with you, or check in with the caregiver every half an hour or so.

Leaving your child with other caregivers is also a valuable way to help your child feel comfortable with other people, which is particularly important if you must be away from your child for an emergency at some point. When my sons were four-and-a-half and two, my stepsister Kim passed away, and my husband and I needed to fly to another city to attend her service. Because our friend Darren had babysat regularly for both boys, we were able to rely on him to take care of our children during our brief absence—making all of us feel more secure during this difficult time. This experience with another caregiver allowed our children to receive care from a familiar and comforting person.

Chapter 11
Sibling Rivalry
and Family Spacing

You might be wondering why in the world this book even has a chapter on adding a new baby, and how that really fits with common child-raising challenges. But many of us do want more than one child, and wonder when the best time might be—for ourselves and for our first-born—to add a second child. This is a common concern, in part because we want our kids to be close, but we also want to minimize sibling rivalry. This chapter describes some of the costs and benefits of different approaches to spacing kids for you to consider so that you can do what works best for your family.

THE CHALLENGE OF BECOMING A FAMILY OF FOUR (OR MORE)

Parents who choose to have kids very close together—meaning less than two years apart—are often motivated by a strong desire to get the "bad stuff"—diapers, sleepless nights, teething—out of the way. Others choose close spacing as a way of shortening mom's absence from the work force. Close spacing is also chosen by couples who want their kids close in age so they are more likely to share interests, and find some of the same activities entertaining. Any or all of these factors, separately or in combination, can lead parents to choose to have kids close in age.

WHY VERY CLOSE SPACING IS HARD ON YOUR KIDS . . . AND YOU

Although close spacing has its advantages, having kids less than two years apart can lead to a number of short- and long-term consequences, including:

Disrupting the attachment bond. Children who are younger than two don't have the cognitive ability to understand what having a new baby means—from their point of view, all of a sudden a new person is needing constant attention from the very people who used to constantly dote on them! They can't understand why they have to share their mom, or why they have to delay having their own needs met. Although parents may see their one-year-old as highly capable—especially compared to an infant—this is precisely when children are trying to actively engage in and explore their worlds. In turn, they very much need parental help in setting and enforcing consistent boundaries, and serving as a stable base in this brand-new world. If parents can't be readily available to the older child during this crucial stage, that child will experience frustration, anxiety, and even fear.

There is also the emotional stress on moms who have responsibility for two kids who both rely on you to take care of virtually all their needs—feeding, dressing, diaper changing. There will be many times when both kids desperately need attention at the same time, and it's very hard to choose who to take care of first, particularly since neither child is able to understand—or easily tolerate—the delay.

Increasing sibling rivalry. Although closely spaced children do tend to have more in common, this supposed advantage can actually have negative consequences in terms of sibling rivalry. Children who are very close in age do share similar interests and abilities, but also experience greater competition, and, in turn, more sibling rivalry, especially if they are the same sex. Given the realities of recovery from childbirth—especially if a Caesarean was performed—and the demands of breast-feeding an infant, it's very easy to pay more attention to the baby and push the care of the older child onto dad or another caregiver. This, in turn, can increase the child's negative feelings towards a sibling in the early days after birth. What you need to understand is that no matter how good your intentions are, it's inevitable that the older child will be encouraged to be more independent. It can't be helped under these circumstances. For example, changing one child's diapers may not seem like such a task, but once another baby arrives, people may hurry the toilet training process for the older child, (which, as we know from Chapter 7, has numerous long-term consequences.) This, too, can foster sibling rivalry.

Health issues for mom and baby. It is stressful to a woman's body to have less than eighteen months between pregnancies. Pregnancy is hard work, labor is hard work, and nursing is hard work. And a second pregnancy is very different—physically and emotionally—from a first pregnancy. Imagine dealing with the physical and emotional challenges of being pregnant while simultaneously caring for a small child who is still dependent on you—a child who needs to be carried when he or she is too tired to walk, who needs to be lifted onto a changing table or in and out of the bathtub. All of these things are hard to do while pregnant. You are on your feet more—no such thing as spending an easy afternoon in bed. Closely spaced pregnancies are also hard on babies: One study in the *New England Journal of Medicine* found that babies who were conceived within six months of the birth of another child were 30 percent more likely to be born premature.

Creates unnecessary expenses. Sure, money shouldn't be the main reason you decide to delay having a second child, but it is much more expensive to have two kids close in age simply because you don't benefit from many hand-me-downs. If your first child is still in a crib, you need to buy a new crib. If your first child still can't walk independently, you need to buy a double stroller. If your first child still needs a high chair, you need to buy a second high chair. You see what I mean. And this isn't just for the short-term: You'll have two kids needing braces at about the same time, then before you know it they'll be needing a car and going to college!

WHY SPACING CHILDREN A FEW YEARS APART HAS LONG-TERM ADVANTAGES

Deciding to wait to get pregnant until your child is at least two has a number of advantages:

It enhances the attachment bond. Children who have had two or three years of being an only child will be confident in your love and less threatened about sharing that love with a sibling because they have had time to form a secure attachment with you.

It minimizes jealousy. Because older kids have already had their time alone with mom and dad and have learned that their needs must sometimes wait, they are less likely to experience high levels of jealousy towards a new baby. In fact, they are more likely to empathize with the baby's need for you precisely because they understand the comfort a parent provides. After hearing many of my friends warn me about the jealousy of their first-born towards their younger sibling, I was quite prepared for my older son, Andrew, who was two-and-a-half when his brother was born, to become particularly needy of me when his younger brother, Robert, cried. Much to my surprise, however, Andrew was very concerned about comforting Robert—and, if my husband happened to be holding the baby, Andrew would yell, "Give him to Mom, give him to Mom!" Children who are three or older also already have a life outside of the home that no longer consists of just Mom, so the baby is less threatening to their world. Three- and four-year-olds attend preschool, have play dates, and can do many things on their own. All of these factors contribute to an easy adjustment to a new baby.

It's easier for parents. Three-year-olds can do many things independently since they have considerable physical skills. This makes life easier since they need little or no assistance from you in getting dressed, getting into and out of their carseat, walking up and down stairs, feeding themselves, and perhaps even using the toilet. They also have strong verbal skills, so they can talk about their needs and express their feelings as well as understand your explanations. Most importantly, older kids are able and willing to help with the baby—bringing you a clean diaper, making baby smile, and picking up the toy baby has dropped. This helping factor even provides the youngster with a sense of pride and accomplishment.

THE SLOW AND STEADY APPROACH TO INTRODUCING A SIBLING

If you're expecting, here are specific steps to help ease the immediate adjustment and foster good sibling relationships for life:

1. Prepare your child in advance—but not too far in advance.

Kids need to know from you that a sibling is coming, but very small kids don't have much of a sense of time so it is better not to tell them in the first few months—certainly not during your first trimester when your pregnancy won't be obvious. However, you don't want your child to hear about it from someone else, so it is a good idea to share the news with your child early in your second trimester. Part of this preparation means talking in general about what babies are like. This can include talking about your child when he or she was a baby, showing them photos of themselves as a baby, and discussing the day they were born. If you have friends or relatives with babies, try to spend some time with them so that your child can see what a real baby can, and cannot, do. If you are going to nurse, discuss with your child that the baby will drink milk from Mommy's breast, and find books—or, better yet, actual women and babies—that show nursing. If you know the baby's sex, let the older child know—which is a good way of preventing disappointment when the baby arrives and is not his or her preferred sex (or a puppy, which was my own preference when my brother was born!).

2. Make big changes before the baby's arrival.

Adjusting to a new sibling is a major life change for everyone, and especially for kids. Make every effort to keep other things in your child's life stable and predictable. If your older child is starting school, or moving to a "big bed," or giving up a bottle or pacifier, make those changes at least several months—not weeks—before the baby's arrival. This is also a good time to develop a social network of playdates or playgroups if your child doesn't attend a preschool, so that he or she has an independent life outside the home.

3. Involve the older child in preparing for the baby's arrival.

The addition of another child is a family event, so include your older child in planning for the baby's arrival. One way to do this is to give him or her various jobs to complete. They could, for example, help decide where the crib should go, set up the baby monitor, and arrange the baby's toys and books. My sons enjoyed going shopping for particular baby items—sheets, diapers, clothing. Older children can help pack your bag for the hospital (make sure to bring a photo of them) and choose the baby's going home outfit. We included our older child on our birth announcement for his brother, and then both boys on our birth announcement for their sister.

4. Prepare the older child for what will happen when the baby is about to arrive.

Kids are understandably nervous about what will happen when you go to the hospital to give birth, so make sure to explain the process in an understandable way. For example, go over who will be staying with him, or where he will go during this time, and that you will only be away a night or two. Many hospitals run a class for siblings to prepare for the new baby, which can include a tour of the nursery, practice holding (plastic!) babies, and practical information about what babies can and cannot do. My sons both participated in this class before the arrival of their sister, and still refer to information they learned— "Remember to clean up your toys so Caroline doesn't eat your Legos," and "Babies don't have teeth so they can't have apples." Buy some books specifically designed for children who are welcoming a new sibling, such as *Arthur's*

New Baby (by Marc Brown), *Will There Be A Lap For Me?* (by Dorothy Corey and Nancy Poydar), and *A Baby Sister for Frances* (by Russell Hoban and Lillian Hoban).

When the baby arrives bring your older child to the hospital for even a quick visit as soon as possible, for reassurance that you are OK and that you will be home soon. It's important to remember that your child will be much more excited to see you than the baby. Try not to be holding the baby so that you can give your older child your full attention. Tell him that you miss him and you'll be home soon—after all, from his perspective, you are now just spending time alone with the baby. Bring a photo of your older child to the hospital, and have it prominently displayed in your room.

This first visit is also a great time to start creating good will towards the baby. You might want to have a special treat like a snack or a gift (ideally described as a present from the baby) ready for your older child—a great idea described in the book *Twice Blessed* (by Joan Leonard). My older kids still talk about the great garage and car set they "received" at the hospital from their new sister Caroline.

5. Keep the focus on the older child.

When the baby arrives, he or she is obviously going to command a lot of attention from others, including parents, relatives, and friends. Do what you can to keep the focus on the older child, such as asking the older child to "introduce" the baby to visitors, involving him in unwrapping gifts for the baby, and remarking to visitors about the baby's super big brother or sister. Because some people will arrive with gifts only for the baby, it's a good idea to buy and wrap a few inexpensive toys so that he can open a gift whenever one arrives for the baby. Similarly, we bought our older son a new toy chest when his brother was born—to compensate for the new presents that we were buying for the baby.

Spend some time alone with your older child, particularly in the early days and weeks immediately after the baby is born. An outing alone with Mom or Dad can go a long way towards easing resentment towards the baby who seems to be taking up so much parental time and attention. So, take your child to a movie or ballgame, a favorite restaurant, or just to a playground. My husband took our older son, who was then two-and-a-half, for a long ride on a city bus the day after our second son was born—a thrilling event which was remembered fondly for many months.

6. Let your child be involved with the baby . . .
   if he or she wants.

There is no way around it—your household is going to revolve around and focus on the baby. What you should do is include the older children by giving them opportunities to be involved in the baby's care. Sure, there are practical limits to what they can do, but there are many things that even a toddler or preschooler can help with. Be sure you ask them to do things like selecting a diaper for the baby, handing you a towel to use after the baby's bathtime, or showing the baby a toy.

On the other hand, if your child is not interested in interacting with the baby, that's fine. Forcing unwanted interaction only adds to any resentment or jealousy they are feeling.

7. Avoid using the baby as an excuse.

When you are overwhelmed with caring for your newborn, your older child's demands can seem particularly exhausting and irritating. But avoid, at all costs, using the baby as an excuse for not spending time with your older child—what better way to ensure feelings of anger and jealousy? If there are specific times when you are with the baby and your older child always seems to need you, work out viable alternatives. For example, if you are nursing, keep a basket of "special toys" beside you that he or she gets to play with only while you nurse. Another great idea comes from a friend who used nursing time as "video time" for her toddler who thought of it as something special to do with Mom and the baby.

8. Stick to routines.

After the baby arrives, stick to old routines to give your child a sense of stability. If your child attends daycare or preschool, continue to send them each morning, even if you are now staying home with the baby. Kids need the comfort of a familiar routine and you (trust me) will need a break from managing two! You should, however, modify your child's regular routine to incorporate *some* special privileges. Choose whichever changes work well for your family, such as having a (slightly) later bedtime, scheduling a regular outing with Mom or Dad, or attending a movie, play, or sporting event.

9. Get help when you need it.

Going from one child to two is more than twice as much work—and believe me, you are going to need help.

Don't be afraid to rely on friends, relatives, or neighbors, and don't be shy about asking for the help you need. Come up with a list of things that would be helpful and then have a few ideas ready when others ask: Could you spend an hour with the kids in the morning so I can shower; pick up some groceries for me; take the baby for a stroller walk so I can have alone time with my older child? You'll not only get the help you specifically need, but it also makes life easier for your helpers who aren't forced to try and guess what help you want.

If you don't have a family support network nearby, hire some help. One option is to hire a professionally trained postpartum doula, whose job it is to assist moms with bathing, diapering, and feeding the baby, running errands, and helping with household tasks (see the appendix for information on finding a postpartum doula). Doulas receive special training on sibling issues, and can also entertain your older child, or alternatively, take care of the baby while you entertain your child. I used a doula a few hours a week during the first month after the birth of my second and third child, and found it extremely helpful. My insurance plan actually covered the cost of a doula, so check with your health insurance plan to see if free postpartum doula care could be an option for you. Even if it is not covered, hiring a doula for a few hours each week for a few months after the birth is well worth the cost for the peace of mind it will bring you—and your kids.

10. Be tolerant of behavioral changes in your older child.

It's not uncommon for an older child to show some behavioral changes in the weeks and months following the arrival of a sibling. Many children regress, so don't be surprised or concerned if you see behavior such as thumbsucking, bedwetting, or waking up in the middle of the night. Trust me, this stage will pass—just give your child time to adjust to your new family set-up.

Chapter 12
Slow and Steady
Parenting for Life

As parents, we are constantly faced with difficult decisions to make while raising our children. What's more, we're forced to make some of these decisions quickly and in high pressure situations—at the dinner table in front of in-laws or in a crowded line at the grocery store, for instance. It's times like these when we're most tempted to choose short-term solutions. But if we remember that the cost of these short-term choices is just too high, we'll begin making longer-term choices more and more as we begin to experience the power they have to make life better for our children, ourselves, and for the whole family. Over time, these choices will become second nature, because we will see first-hand the benefits of the slow and steady approach. Long-term choices, as we've seen, do more than correct a current situation: They work in the long-run by building our children's self-confidence and self-esteem, enhancing the bond between us and our children, and making our own life simpler and easier.

RECOGNIZING QUICK-FIX APPROACHES IN EVERYDAY LIFE

Although I've focused on the particular challenges parents of babies and toddlers face in this book—sleeping, eating, toilet training, etc.—the benefits of making long-term choices versus short-term choices don't stop at age three. If you learn how to apply the slow and steady parenting approach with your baby and toddler, you can then use this approach when dealing with other common parenting challenges. I hope that the examples I've given have instilled a sense of how to recognize ways that you can use the short-term versus long-term approach to guide your behavior through your daily parenting situations.

APPLYING LONG-TERM ADVANTAGES TO YOUR LIFE

You might think of the long-term choices as daunting, but relax—what I'm simply saying is that you need to understand the short- and long-term consequences of all of the decisions you make in child rearing so that you are able to make the very best choices you can that will help your child to develop and mature to their highest potential. Yes, long-term parenting takes time, but as with all things—from cooking to gardening (or raising kids)— patience, tenderness, attention to detail, a little prodding, and the ability to sit back sometimes and observe go a long way to future success.

This doesn't mean, though, that you must be rigid and only use long-term approaches. After all, this is life, and we are human. Sometimes we make short-term choices because *right at that moment*, that option works best. Here are some examples: I needed some time to make an important work call when I was working at home one day, so I handed my then three-year-old a box of animal crackers, in hopes that he might be occupied enough to avoid interrupting me for thirty minutes (and it worked). I patted my daughter's back for twenty minutes one night trying to get her to sleep, because I was truly desperate to get to sleep myself—and this seemed faster than letting her struggle to fall asleep on her own. And I began to allow one thirty-minute video each afternoon when my older son was four . . . because I desperately needed time to write in order to finish this book!

All of us will at times choose the short-term option, which is admittedly very appealing at the moment, and there's nothing wrong with making such a choice. But you need to be aware that these decisions are choices that are desirable in the short-term, but can lead to long-term consequences. So, make short-term choices if and when you need to, but don't make them out of ignorance (e.g., a belief that formula feeding is basically as good as breast-feeding, or that pacifier use is the best way to soothe your child, or that television is really educational for a toddler). You need to make decisions that are right for you, but you can make the best decisions that will affect the future life of you and your child only when you have a full awareness of the short- and long-term advantages and consequences. In sum, ignorance is not bliss—and knowledge is power.

APPENDIX

Relevant Books

Christopherson, E. R., and S. L. Mortweet. *Parenting That Works: Building Skills That Last A Lifetime.* Washington, DC: APA Press, 2003.

Crain, W. *Reclaiming Childhood: Letting Children Be Children In Our Achievement-Oriented Society.* New York: Times Books, 2003.

Hirsk-Pasek, K., R. M. Golinkoff, and D. Eyer. *Einstein Never Used Flash Cards: How Our Children REALLY Learn—and Why They Need to Play More and Memorize Less.* Emmaus, PA: Rodale Press, 2004.

Leonard, J. *Twice Blessed: Everything You Need to Know About Having a Second Child—Preparing Yourself, Your Marriage, and Your Firstborn for a New Family of Four.* New York: St. Martin's Press, 2000.

Winn, M. *The Plug-In Drug: Television, Computers, and Family Life.* New York: Penguin Books, 2002.

Relevant Organizations

La Leche League International (LLLI). Website: http://www.lalecheleague. org. Address: 1400 N. Meacham Road, Schaumburg, IL 60173-4808 Phone: (847) 519-7730

National Association of Postpartum Care Services. Website: http://www.napcs. org. Address: 800 Detroit Street, Denver, CO 80206. Phone: (800) 453-6852. Email: DoulaCare@napcs.org.

References

Affonso, D.D., V. Wahlberg, and B. Persson. 1989. Exploration of mothers' reactions to the kangaroo method of prematurity care. *Neonatal Network, 7,* 43-51

Anderson, G. C. 1991. Current knowledge about skin-to-skin (kangaroo) care for preterm infants. *Journal of Perinatology, 11,* 216-226.

Arnold, D. H., L. McWilliams, and E. H. Arnold. 1998. Teacher discipline and child misbehavior in daycare: Untangling causality with correlational data. *Developmental Psychology, 34,* 276-287.

Bernal, J., and M. P. Richards. 1970. The effects of bottle and Breast-Feeding on infant development. *Journal of Psychosomatic Research, 14,* 247-252.

Blum, N. J., B. Taubman, and N. Nemeth. 2003. Relationship between age at initiation of toilet training and duration of training: A prospective study. *Pediatrics, 111,* 810-814.

Chase-Lansdale, P. L., and M. T. Owen. 1987. Maternal employment in a family context: Effects on infant-mother and infant-father attachments. *Child Development, 58,* 1505-1512.

Dettling, A. C., M. R. Gunnar, and B. Donzella. 1999. Cortisol levels of young children in full-day childcare centers: Relations with age and temperament. *Psychoneuroendocrinology, 24,* 519-536.

DiLalla, L. F. 1998. Daycare, child, and family influences on preschoolers' social behaviors in a peer play setting. *Child Study Journal, 28,* 223-244.

Egeland, B., and M. Hiester. 1995. The long-term consequences of infant daycare and mother-infant attachment. *Child Development, 66,* 474-485.

Fisher, J. O., and L. L. Birch. 1999. Restricting access to foods and children's eating. *Appetite, 32,* 405-419.

Fisher, J. O., and L. L. Birch. 1999. Restricting access to palatable foods affects children's behavioral response, food selection, and intake. *American Journal of Clinical Nutrition, 69,* 1264-1272.

Fleming, A. S., D. N. Ruble, G. L. Flett, and D. L. Shaul. 1988. Postpartum adjustment in first-time mothers: Relations between mood, maternal attitudes, and mother-infant interactions. *Developmental Psychology, 24,* 71-81.

Fox, A., and C. Schaefer. 1996. Pacifier use in young children: Practical research findings. *Psychology: A Journal of Human Behavior, 33,* 30-34.

Gale, G., L. Franck, and C. Lund. 1993. Skin-to-skin (kangaroo) holding of the intubated premature infant. *Neonatal Network, 12,* 49-57.

Hastings, P. D., and J. E. Grusec. 1998. Parenting goals as organizers of responses to parent-child disagreement. *Developmental Psychology, 34,* 465-479.

Hu, F. B., T. Y., Li, G. A., Codlitz, W. C. Willet, and J. E. Manson. 2003. Television watching and other sedentary behaviors in relation to risk of obesity and type 2 diabetes mellitus in women. *Journal of the American Medical Association, 289,* 1785-1791.

Huesmann, L. R., J. Moise-Titus, C. L. Podolski, and L. D. Eron. 2003. Longitudinal relations between children's exposure to TV violence and their aggressive and violent behavior in young adulthood: 1977-1992. *Developmental Psychology, 39,* 201-221.

Huston, A. C., J. C. Wright, and J. Marquis. 1999. How young children spend their time: Television and other activities. *Developmental Psychology, 35,* 912-925.

Kopp, C. B. 1989. Regulation of distress and negative emotions: A developmental view. *Developmental Psychology, 25,* 343-354.

Legendre, A. U. 2003. Environmental features influencing toddlers' bioemotional reactions in daycare centers. *Environment & Behavior, 35,* 523-549.

Mennella, J. A., C. P. Jagnow, and G. K. Beauchamp. 2001. Prenatal and postnatal flavor learning by human infants. *Pediatrics, 107,* E88.

NICHD Early Child-Care Research Network. 1997. The effects of infant child-care on infant-mother attachment security: Results of the NICHD study of early childcare. *Child Development, 68,* 860-879.

Mumme, D. L., and A. Fernald. 2003. The infant as onlooker: Learning from emotional reactions observed in a television scenario. *Child Development, 74*, 221-237.

Parpal, M. and E. E. Maccoby. 1985. Maternal responsiveness and subsequent child compliance. *Child Development, 56*, 1326-1334.

Robinson, T. N. 1999. Reducing children's television viewing to prevent obesity: A randomized controlled trial. *Journal of the American Medical Association, 282*, 1561-1567.

Story, M., and P. Faulkner. 1990. The prime-time diet: A content analysis of eating behavior and food messages in television programs and commercials. *American Journal of Public Health, 80,* 738-740.

Wahler, R. G., and J. J. Fox. 1980. Solitary toy play and time out: A family treatment package for children with aggressive and oppositional behavior. *Journal of Applied Behavior Analysis, 13,* 23-39.

Watamura, S. E., B. Donzella, J. Alwin, and M. R. Gunnar. 2003. Morning-to-afternoon increases in cortisol concentrations for infants and toddlers at childcare: Age differences and behavioral correlates. *Child Development, 74*, 1006-1020.

Westerman, M. A. 1990. Coordination of maternal directives with preschoolers' behavior in compliance-problem and healthy dyads. *Developmental Psychology, 26*, 621-630.

Wiesenfeld, A. R., C. Z. Malatesta, P. B. Whitman, C. Granrose, and R. Uili. 1985. Psychophysiological response of breast- and bottle-feeding mothers to their infants' signals. *Psychophysiology, 22*, 79-86.

INDEX

NOTES

ABOUT THE AUTHOR

Catherine A. Sanderson is an Associate Professor of Psychology at Amherst College. She received a BA in psychology, with a specialization in Health and Development, from Stanford University in 1990, and a PhD in psychology from Princeton University in 1997. Dr. Sanderson's research examines how personality and social variables influence health related behaviors such as safer sex and disordered eating, the development of persuasive messages and interventions to prevent unhealthy behavior, and the predictors of relationship satisfaction. This research has received grant funding from the National Science Foundation and the National Institute of Health. Dr. Sanderson has published over twenty-five journal articles and book chapters, has written a college textbook on Health Psychology, and teaches step aerobics in her "free time." She is married to Bart Hollander, and is the mother of Andrew (age 7), Robert (age 4), and Caroline (age 1). Her hobbies include reading fiction, eating chocolate, and watching *The Bachelor*.